Class Consciousness in the Novels of KAMALA MARKANDAYA

PRAVATI MISRA

ATLANTIC

ATLANTIC PUBLISHERS AND DISTRIBUTORS

Published by
ATLANTIC PUBLISHERS AND DISTRIBUTORS
B-2, Vishal Enclave, Opp. Rajouri Garden, New Delhi-27
Phones : 5413460, 5429987

Sales Office
4215/1, Ansari Road, Darya Ganj, New Delhi-02
Phones : 3273880, 3285873, 3280451
Fax : 91-11-3285873
e-mail : info@atlanticbooks.com
web site : www.atlanticbooks.com

ISBN 81-269-0001-6

Typeset at
APD Computer Graphics, Delhi

Printed in India at
Mehra Offset Press, Delhi

Dedicated in Fond Memory of
My Late Parents :

DIBYASINGHA MISRA

and

CHANCHALA MISRA

PREFACE

This book aims at an evaluation of the novels of Kamala Markandaya in the perspective of class-consciousness embedded in her fictional narrative. The study attempts to explore the impact of class-consciousness on the attitudes, manners and conditions of living in the context of modern India as it moves from a conservative and traditional social order to a liberal and urbanized socio-economic and cultural ethos. It seeks to explore Markandaya's concern with the predicament of the individual in a class-ridden society subjected to a process of radical change. The book attempts to substantiate the hypothesis that in the process of this change, the self confronts tensions, uncertainties and conflicts that lead to deep psychological and spiritual wounds. The self, with its desires, instincts and dreams, encounters a world of reality governed by social, economic and cultural forces. This encounter leads to a crisis of identity. The self tries to surmount this crisis through resistance or reconciliation, through protest or surrender. In this process of self's grappling with reality, there is anguish and suffering. This study, in short, is an attempt at exploring the paradox of human condition in terms of conflict between self and society, between free will and necessity.

While Kamala Markandaya's novels reflect a general preoccupation with class consciousness represented in almost all major Indian novels in English, her fictional world has nevertheless a direct pattern governed by an intense perception of anguish in a class ridden society in the process of radical transition. This book has been written with the full awareness of the huge quantity of critical writing on Kamala Markandaya. While it is presumptuous to claim absolute originality, this book can nevertheless claim originality in terms of a fresh organization of various perceptions and interpretations. In the process of this reorganization the book hopes to illuminate a perspective, which is central to the understanding and appeal of Kamala Markandaya's fiction.

I express my deep gratitude to Dr. Susama Tej, ex-principal, R.D. Women's College, Bhubaneswar for her valuable guidance and constant inspiration.

Words would be hardly adequate to express my thanks and gratitude to Prof. J.N. Patnaik of Utkal University, Vanivihar but for whose help and encouragement this work could not have been completed.

I take this opportunity to express my thanks to my husband Er N.C. Dash, Managing Director, Southern Electricity Supply Company of Orissa Limited without whose inspiration, moral support and timely help, the work could not have been possible. I am also thankful to my son-in-law, Tapas, daughter, Pranati, son, Pranab, Dr. D.P. Choudhury and Dr. B.K. Das who have helped me in several ways.

I am extremely thankful to my stenographers Mr. R. Appala Raju and Mr. B. Kameswar Rao for their co-operation. I am grateful to all my friends and well wishers who have helped me in the completion of the project.

PRAVATI MISRA

CONTENTS

1

Classes and Attitudes

The structure of Indian Society has always been governed by a delicate relationship among its classes stratified according to economic status and social roles. From the pre-colonial past to the post-colonial present, India has always retained some form of class-distinction based on caste and wealth. Today while the traditional system of caste is fast eroding, there still exists an insistent distinction based on economic and political power. In terms of this distinction, the Indian society can broadly be classified into three hierarchical levels; the working class, the middle class and the upper class. Though each of the economic classes tends to assure a distinctive identity *vis-à-vis* its social status and functions, it is not always true that the three classes have very clear and defined boundaries. While the very soul of the working class and the middle class is their aspiration for an upward mobility, the upper class is vastly diverse in terms of life-style, attitudes and social functions. The novels of Kamala Markandaya offer a wide spectrum of characters, places and situations which not only center round the controlling forces of the three classes but also reflect their joys and sorrows, agony and anguish as they negotiate with the challenges and complexities of life and living. In this chapter, a modest attempt has been made to identify the presence of these three classes in Kamala Markandaya's novels, not only as distinct social groups but also as inter-acting and contradictory forces that determine the relationship between self and society.

II

Interestingly, Kamala Markandaya's early impulse to write fiction coincides with her deep concern with the poverty and squalor, conflicts and suffering, dreams and aspirations of the down-trodden class. Two of her early novels *The Nectar in a Sieve* and *A Handful of Rice* contain symbolic portraits of the starving millions, the exploited working class who struggle desperately for bare subsistence both in the rural and the urban areas. Unlike the African novelists Chinua Achebe, Wole Soyinka and Carribean writer V.S. Naipaul who reflect a deep sense of frustration at the disintegration of old order and at the loss of traditional values, Kamala Markandaya shows her firm confidence on the unflinching spirit of the Indian social order to sustain itself through the worst of trails and tribulations. As Uma Parameswaran rightly observes :

> It is easy to wring tears of pity for the plight of the peasant, underfed, uneducated, exploited and easier still to rouse anger and contempt for the superstitious and slow-moving masses. They stand there vulnerable and open to every attack, be it indifference, contempt, or emasculating charity. But to evoke admiration, even envy, for the simple faith and unswerving tenacity they hold needs sympathy and skill. Kamala Markandaya has both (92).

Nectar in a Sieve is a vivid record of the hungry rural peasantry whose life is afflicted by the existing social institutions and rituals such as child marriage, widowhood, negligence of female child, slavery, landlessness, homelessness, casteism and illiteracy. The novel centers round the acutely suffering poor tenant farmer Nathan and his wife Rukmani, the narrator of the tale. They represent thousands of uprooted peasants under the pressure of industrialism and landlordism. Among the rural folk, there is a clear dichotomy between the upper class, the landlords and the money lenders on the one hand and the poor tenant farmers and the labouring class on the other. Rukmani gives a graphic picture of the farmers' life of hardships, of fear and of hunger :

> This is one of the truths of our existence as those

> who live by the land know; that some times we eat and sometimes we starve. We live by our labours from one harvest to the next, there is no certain telling whether we shall be able to feed ourselves and our children, and if bad times are prolonged we know we must see the weak surrender their lives and this fact, too, is within our experience. In our life there is no margin for misfortune (136).

People generally learn to live out this misery with calm acquiescence until the onset of real disaster on the land as well as the rural economy when a tennery is set up in the neighbouring area. It starts expanding by acquiring cultivable lands of the village. It disturbs the apparently calm and peaceful life of the village. In addition to this man-made menace, when nature acts as a hostile force in the form of draught and flood resulting in failure of crops, the tenant farmers are forced into starvation, Heavy storm causes havoc to the poor farmer but the tannery stands unaffected, and cement holding it together, despite the raging winds; but the workers huts, of more flimsy construction, were 'now only a heap of mud with heir owners' possessions studding them in a kind of pitiless decoration' (45-46).

The ruthless landlords and the merciless money lenders hardly care to come to the rescue of the starving poor farmers. As a result, they are evicted from their beloved land. When all their saving is consumed, Nathan and Rukmani approach, Hanuman, the rice merchant who heartlessly rejects their prayer for rice. Then they come to Biswas, the money lender, for rice in exchange of their two silver coins. But he rebukes them demanding more, "Take it or leave it. I can get double that sum from the tanners' (47). This is the curse that the tannery brings to the poor villagers. Nathan pitifully laments :

> Now the landlord can wring from us his moneys and care not for the misery he evokes, for indeed it would be difficult for any man to see another starve and his wife and children as well; or to enjoy the profits born of such travail (77).

The only protesting and rebellious voice against social inequality and injustice is raised by the compassionate English Missionary doctor Kennington. He expresses his disgust at the Indian poor peasants' passivity. He asks Rukmani, why do you keep this ghastly silence? 'Why do you not demand — cry out for help — do something?' (47-48). But the villagers cannot cope with the changing social situations. The industrial resurgence snatches not only their land and property but also their sons, promising them employment and better financial prospects. The exodus of the rural people to the urban areas contributes to the congestion in the cities, pollution of the environment and imbalance in the distribution of population.

The picture of social inequality, exploitation of the poor and unhealthy consequences of urbanization has been painted in Venkatramani's *Murugan, the Tiller* (1927), Mulk Raj Anand's *Coolie* (1936), Bhabani Bhattacharya's *So Many Hungers* (1947) and *He Who Rides a Tiger* (1954). A.N. Dwivedi and Niroj Banerjee comment on Kamala Markandaya's realistic study of such pitiable figures, 'At best, she is a novelist of sensitive individuals placed in certain piquant situations and of their ensuing actions and reactions in the given social and cultural context' (131).

Kamala Markandaya shows that not only Nathan's family but the whole community undergoes similar afflictions. The working class suffers mostly for the economic disproportion, malpractices adopted by the crooked and the social changes difficult to be accepted by the tradition-bound rural people. Rukmani's father is a headman of his village. He spends lavishly on the nuptial ceremony of his elder daughters. When Rukmani's turn comes, his administrative power has been shifted from himself to the newly appointed revenue collector as a result of which his financial position gets deteriorated. He is unable to meet the demand of the rich grooms. Hence, he hands his youngest daughter Rukmani over to Nathan, a poor tenant farmer. The early years of their married life pass peacefully and lovingly with the produce they earn from their labour on the Zamindar's land. With the failure of crops due to inclement weather, Nathan cannot feed his enlarged family of six children. Rukmani blames the tannery which invades the fertile, cultivable land. The children's playground also has been invaded. The market price has been raised sky high. The din and bustle has swept away the peace and calm of the village. The price hike has also affected farmers' wives, Kali, Kunti and the shopkeeper's wife Janaki. Their common grief of starvation and undernourished state has been expressed in the complaint Rukmani makes against the tannery establishment. She says, "No sugar or dhal or ghee have we tasted since they came, and should have had none, so long as they remained" (32).

There is a perceptible shift of socio-economic activity from land to factory and from village to city. The village shopkeeper Perumal, Janaki's husband, cannot compete with the shopkeepers who hail from the town. She is bound to close his shop. The grownup boys, Kunti's son and Rukamani's sons Arjun and Thambi join the factory. They leave their paternal profession of tilling the land for better financial prospects. Thumbi explains their stand to his father, "If it were your land, or mine, I would work with you gladly. But what profit to labour for another and get so little in return? Far better to turn away for such injustice" (56).

When the demand of the youngsters for higher wages is not fulfilled by the tannery they start for Ceylon to work in the tea plantation. Rukmani's third son Raja is killed with the charge of theft. The youngest son Kuti dies of starvation. The family gets the biggest shock of disintegration. It is only Selvam who stays back to work in Kenny's hospital. Nathan and Rukmani start for the city with the hope of meeting their son Murugan. But he is lost in the concrete jungle of the city. They break stones in the quarry to earn their livelihood. In the temple their belongings are stolen. Thus, disillusioned with the urban world with all its menace of indifference, theft and treachery, they finally decide to return home. But being exposed to cold, hunger and old age, Nathan collapses on the road and dies leaving Rukmani forlorn. Despite all her suffering, her solitary struggle against all odds, she returns to the village with the leper boy Puli with the hope of curing him in Kenny's hospital. What she convinces her only surviving son, Selvam and daughter, Ira is given in the quotation from Coleridge, 'Work without hope draws Nectar in a Sieve/ And hope without an object cannot live.' Ira and Selvam become objects of her hope in life, Observing Nathan and Rukmani as symbols of teeming millions, Hari Mohan Prasad comments :

> It is an epic of the Indian life at the grassroots, a full view of the village world where peasants grow and live, suffer and endure and emerge more dignified, more human in their elements with their tattered rags, their dying means and their obstinate clinging to the soil like the stump withered all over but its roots delved in the earth (98).

In this bleak picture of Indian social life the darkest zone is the neglected poor women. In the male dominated society a woman, however, sacrificing and painstaking, is not allowed the right to freedom of speech and human dignity. The women labourers are paid lower wages than men. They are subject to exploitation and oppression because of their ignorance and innocence. Rukmani's daughter Ira gets married to a peasant boy at the age of fourteen. But she is abandoned by her husband five years after their marriage because she fails to beget a child. Thus, she is thrown to a life of degradation and debasement. She does not mind getting corrupted, adopting prostitution with the hope of feeding her little brother Kuti. Nathan's fatherly ego is wounded. He feels shocked at the disheartening sight of Ira's coming home late at night. He helplessly protests against the shameful situation 'I will not have it said. I will not have you parading at night.' But Rukmani, as a mother can neither protest nor object. She quietly endures as she did in her youth when Nathan had extra marital relations with Kunti. She explains passively, 'So we got used to her comings and goings, as we had got used to so much else' (104).

Ira is corrupt in the conventional sense but she can at least buy rice, salt and milk for the sick child. Even though the child dies of undernourishment, Ira's sacrifice and sincere efforts can never be denied. Rukmani accepts this life of suffering as inevitable. When Dr. Kenny asserts, "there is no grandeur in want or in endurance" she replies passively and ironically, 'Want is our companion from birth to death, familiar as the seasons or the earth, varying only in degree' (115).

Rukmani, though literate, is not free from the prejudice against the girl child. Her reaction at the sight of the first born is, 'what woman wants a girl for her first born' (19). She sheds tears of weakness and disappointment. Like all Indian women who cherish to be mothers of sons, she is aware of her husband's desire for a son "to continue his line and walk beside him on the land" (20). Moreover, a daughter becomes a burden to the family because of the dowry system. Rukmani herself is the victim who is given in marriage to a landless labour because her father is unable to find a better groom for lack of wealth to afford good dowry. Rukmani has to face the wrath of the moneylender, the threatening of the landlord for eviction from land and the indifferent attitude of the city dwellers. The only consoling soul she discovers is in Dr. Kenny, the symbol of civilized man's generosity and broadmindedness. Out of compassion for the rural poor, he establishes a hospital. K.R. Chandrasekharan points out how Kamala Markandaya projects in the English doctor "a good missionary and philanthropic spirit doing his best for a backward country without ostentation or vanity. He is also a neutral observer of life in India" (324).

Rukmani returns to her native place with a new self-awareness, new wisdom of the world obtained from her bitter experiences in the city whose unfortunate product is Puli, the leper boy. Like Synges' Maurya and the Christian Job, she remains calm and composed amidst all losses and sufferings. The novel ends with the return of the native, the glorious figure of the mother sorrow. The sight of her village gives life and enlightenment to her starving and withered spirit. All her past experiences recede into a gloomy reverie.

While *Nectar in a Sieve* is the story of the rural poor, *A Handful of Rice* is that of the urban poor. In both the novels Kamala Markandaya has delineated the story of migration from the rural to the industrial urban centers. As Rukmani's sons shift to the city for their sustenance Ravi, the protagonist, also joins the exodus to the city as the village has nothing to offer him. But to his disappointment the city too has nothing great to offer. As he reflects, "It is the drag round the streets and the searching and the wait and the frustration and bearing the pinpricks that the haughty rich always had in plenty for the poor which he had not been able to endure" (27). Ravi in his struggle for survival meets a gang of anti-socials led by Damodar, the underworld don.

He steals from a tailor's shop and is caught, held up and punished by the tailor Apu and his wife Jayamma. They take pity on the hungry man, and offer him the job of an apprentice in the shop.

Like Dickens' protagonists Oliver Twist, David Copperfield and Pip who depend on their benefactors, Ravi also gets a secure foothold in Apu's house. He works as an apprentice in tailoring. Soon he gets involved in love with Apu's daughter, Nalini, gets married to her and becomes a part of Apu's family. After marriage he decides to lead a respectable life as Apu's son-in-law, terminating his old criminal associations. After Apu's death he assumes the dignified position of the master of the household. But the heavy burden of the entire house, the cost of maintenance of the family and of the in-laws, high price of all commodities, force him into heavy debt. he expresses his disgust and disappointment at his poor and unprivileged condition :

> The city was so crowded, rents so high, that even men with decent incomes searched for years, squashing themselves and their families on to which ever relative had managed to secure foothold in some house. It was a little easier for single men, but even sharing a room would cost ten or twelve rupees a month, too big a slice to take out of the twenty he earned (48).

In addition to Ravi's misery due to the responsibility of maintaining a large family of his in laws, the growth of the textile mill and machine productions also poses threat to his tailoring trade. He can no more satisfy the rich European ladies' demand for the latest dress fashion. He is enraged with the rich ladies who scold him using all insulting and abusive words. He cannot sleep at night thinking of the injustice and humiliations afflicted on him. Coming back home he beats up Nalini mercilessly. Next day he repents for the bruise he has caused to her. Nalini silently suffers her aggrieved husband's anger with downcast looks, heavy heart and tensed mind. Day by day, his financial position deteriorates. With his meager earning and rising prices he can hardly meet all his household expenditure. He cannot repay the loans, cannot pay for light and water, cannot buy medicine for his sick son Raju who dies of inadequate treatment

After Raju's death, Ravi feels helpless, worried and depressed. He thinks of Damodar who might advise him or help him in his disaster. But Damodar sheers at him, "Go back to your village. It is more your size, you are not fit for anything else" (214). Ravi is agonized by a state of ambivalence between need for money and the conscience that would free him from Damodar's grip. He is condemned as a coward, unsuccessful man, unfit for city life as he cannot act violently with the agitated mob, loot the granary and become the unholy hero of the day. He withdraws his aggressive mood when he feels convinced that with violence as a weapon nothing positive can be achieved. Thus, the novel ends with a note of defeat and despair. Ravi accepts defeat by withdrawing himself from Damodar's impious world of glamour and luxury. In spite of his shattered ambitions he restrains himself from undertaking violent rebellious actions. *A Handful of Rice,* as R.K. Srivastava says, is thus, "a pathetic cry of protest of a hungry and anguished half grown child groping for a path haltingly through the labyrinthine lanes of quixotic dreams and ugly realities, rural poverty and urban plenty, but reaching no where" (Symbolic, 174).

Markandaya presents, in her first two novels, a general scene of exodus and the effect of socio-economic changes on the emerging new generations of people. Young men like Murugan and Ravi leave their village with the hope of better living in the town. But their migration leads to unemployment, frustration and immorality. The older generation like Nathan, Rukmani and Ravi's father accept suffering but the younger generation cannot submit themselves to fate. Ravi protests, 'The pattern must have gone on a long time, for generations, because no body objected, nobody protested, they just kept going on and on' (12). He sarcastically points out how the traditional pattern of honest living leads them to go without food, without wealth and health. He is not only affected by the rural poverty but also by the urban moral sickness. A.K. Srinivas Rao aptly remarks on this moral depravity :

> Markandaya is not content with mere fatalistic poetic explanations of human misery; nor is she satisfied with

> a survey of the surfacial situations of social injustice and economic inequility that continue to plague our society. She seeks to probe rather deeper into the moral dilemma that an individual is forced to face in a developing country (226).

The disintegration of Ravi's family is a personal calamity but his rage against social discrimination, against exploitation of the poor highlights the moral chaos of urban life. Like Nathan's family, Ravi's family also disintegrates with the growing success of the textile shop, "Eve." Both Rukmani and Ravi develop a spirit of rebellion at a time of transition when Indian villages are tossed by industrial winds and menaced by urban influences. As Kai Nicholson remarks :

> In the depiction of the Mahanagar and the paddy fields Mrs Markandaya is by far the best exponent. In *A Handful of Rice* and *Nectar in a Sieve* she has, with pointed clarity, portrayed life in its more gruesome and degrading form, undoubtedly her realism is purposeful, and her intention is to awaken polite society to the real problem (120).

'The gruesome and degrading form' of life is not only found in the two early novels but also is crucial constituent in some of her later novels. In her fourth novel *Possession* Kamala Markandaya has delineated the life of the destitute through the depiction of East-West confrontation. Caroline, a young British widow, comes to visit India. She meets a fourteen year old boy, Valmiki, a talented painter in a south Indian village, when she is in search of a local alcoholic drink Arakh. Val is poor and neglected in his undeveloped rural background. He paints on the rocky walls of the caves near his village. All he possesses to pursue his hobby are 'pots and pans and jars, broken saucers, sea-shells and coconut shell halves' (P-14). When Caroline discovers his wasted, uncared for talent, she immediately makes up her mind to take him to London or Paris. When she approaches his parents, they initially refuse to spare their son, for they need him to work on land and for rearing the goats. Caroline tempts them by offering five thousand rupees as a compensation for the loss of the working boy. The financial offer is quite alluring for the family of four sons and four daughters.

However, the village school master feels the business of buying and selling of human being quite unjust while Caroline presumes that she has been successful in possessing Val.

In spite of being trained in the metropolitan fashion, Val feels himself as a permanent outsider in the sophisticated London society. For his poor, half-starved family, his art has no relevance. Though Caroline's prosperous material possessions easily attract the boy, he gradually realizes that he is no more than a diamond in her necklace. All the name and fame he earns is only incidental, as he is exploited to enrich Caroline and satisfy her mundane desires. Being extremely poor and illiterate, he becomes a parasite on his patroness. He totally surrenders himself to her whims and passions. Initially he cannot take any decision by himself. He only follows the courses and the programmes framed by Caroline. He goes to the west at a very delicate stage of growth, when women, wealth and glamour all easily attract him. Caroline has initiated him into sexual and carnal pleasures distracting him from creative pleasures and free play of his imagination. All his inborn skill has been commercialized. He feels suffocated in the materialistic world of affluence. Val complains :

> She does not care for me. She cares only for what I can do and if I do it well it is like one more diamond she can put on the necklace round her throat for her friends to admire, but when I do nothing, I am nothing to her, no more than a small insect in a small crane in the ground (56).

In fact, Caroline has given him freedom from want and poverty, but she stifles his spontaneous activities by demanding returns. Now he realizes that he is worse than the neglected goat-herd. Caroline shows indifference to his needs, his emotions and future prospects. He is mercilessly denied any contact with his family. During his absence, his mother dies a slow death of consumption when she is hardly thirty. With Caroline's bewitching power he feels uprooted from his soil. There is an experience of emotional alienation and suppression. His instinctive love for Ellie and Annabel has been smothered. Finally, he realizes Caroline's selfish motives of aggressive possession. When he tries to free himself from her clutches she tries her best to bring him back to herself. Finally, he returns to his cave in his native Indian village, with an acute awareness of the shallow worldly glory based on money, power, fame, sex and travel. He seems to realize that art is a spontaneous experience, not a commercial deal. R. S. Singh rightly observes :

> Caroline was unable to accept self-expression as the purpose of art, and therefore was unable to see and appreciate this revelation of the inner self of Valmiki in his later paintings. She saw him only as a wasted man, wasting his work in the wilderness of India (25).

Anasuya, the narrator, feels sorry for Caroline, Though Caroline puts an end to Val's starved existence, she cannot realize that the Indian ethos in which the Swamy lives and promotes spiritual awakening is the natural habitation and background for the natural prodigy Valmiki. His artistic talent is promoted smoothly under the benign influence of the enthralling and captivating Swamy. Caroline is portrayed as a contrast to Raja Rao's heroine Madeleine in *The Serpent and the Rope*. Madeleine is refined and culturally advanced. She never tries to possess Rama, but helps him in his spiritual pursuit. However, Val is ultimately dispossessed from Caroline's insensible, relentless grip. She is aggrieved and frustrated in the end in her futile attempt to possess Val whole-heartedly.

In her earlier works Kamala Markandaya exposes the sufferings of individual characters such as Rukmani, Nathan, Ravi, Nalini and Valmiki, who like the tragic characters Tess, Jude and Henchard in Hardy's memorable classic novels, suffer on account of the incursions of industrialization on human values and relationships. The peasants and the rural folk get deprived of their traditional means of income. Both natural calamities and human exploitation of the poor force the villagers to move to industrial and urban centers. They leave their native place in desperate quest for survival and security while there is an inevitable sense of anguish at being displaced from their cultural roots nourished by human values. In her sixth novel The *Coffer Dams*, Markandaya explores the possibility of a reconciliation between human values and industrial progress.

The Coffer Dams presents the incursions of Western technology into a tribal village in South India. The story is based on the construction of a dam on a turbulent river of a South Indian hilly region. As Harish Raizada observes :

> In *The Coffer Dams* (1969) Kamala Markandaya treats a new aspect of the East-West confrontation by depicting the conflict between technological power and the forces of nature symbolized by the turbulent South Indian river which thunders through the jungle and inaccessible gorges of hills around. On the human level the conflict manifests itself in the form of hostility between sophisticated British technicians and the hill-tribesmen of India, who have been dislodged from the site of the dam and who worship the river as a veritable god (58).

The Chief Architects Howard Clinton and Machendrick, British Engineers, work relentlessly against many odds caused by ravages of nature and the hostile attitudes of Krishna, the leader of Indian technicians and workers. The tribal are portrayed as innocent, ignorant, hard working and passive. Their basic need of food and shelter is obtained from the forest itself. Their luxury items include some tin cans, cardboard boots, scented pig's grease for their hair which they collect from the camp shop. The Britishers observe how the tribal are used to the vagaries of life. When they are asked to vacate their land for the camp of the British officers, they hardly resist or protest. Clinton considers the tribe as symbolizing 'the severe retardation of its civilization' and the tribal as the blank opacities of their total incomprehension (35). Clinton convinces himself that he is carrying 'the white man's burden' (156) to elevate the local backward tribesmen.

The British are very sensitive about their social hierarchy. According to their social status, separate provision is made for the officers and their families. The technicians are placed in the subordinate cadre. The big bungalows need large space which needs the dislodgement of the tribes. The poor labourers who 'rattled around like peas in a tin' (104) are seduced away by wages, jobs and bribes. When the river gets wild, crops are swayed away, huts are destroyed, Clinton never expresses his concern for the suffering workers. As V.D. Katamble aptly says,

"The ruthless British Engineer Clinton symbolizes the state of mastership. Whenever he is reported about the labour trouble on the project site, he reacts very sharply and sarcastically" (57). Clinton is an example of the Western pragmatist devoid of any humanistic concern. He is convinced that in grand undertakings, individuals may be sacrificed for a larger cause.

In contrast to Clinton, his wife Helen has been characterized as a sympathetic British soul like Dr. Kenny in *Nectar in a Sieve*. She perceives a total lack of communication between the master builder and the workers. The death of forty labourers in a dynamite blast has been paid no attention too. Clinton suggests that the bodies might have stuck in the rock and hence may be incorporated into the structure. He is callous about the tribal crane operator, Bashiam who is forced to operate the defective crane. Clinton's indifference for the tribal worker's well-being and safety leads to the accident that renders him permanently crippled. Observing such inhuman attitude Helen gets annoyed with her husband. She is human, soft-hearted and compassionate towards the tribals. Like Kenny, she is disturbed at the passivity of the Indian poor and backward class. She discovers natural springs of social intercourse that promote cultural values and fellow feeling. She feels the need for protecting the tribal and promoting a sense of respectability among them. Thus, she plays the role of a rebel and tries her best to remove the bitterness of racial discrimination.

The poor tribals are ill-treated not only by the English, but also by the Indians. Das looks down upon "the naked barbaric savages" (71). Like Helen, Krishnan and Mackendrick are kind towards the downtrodden workers. Helen supplies these passive sufferers with food. Her intimacy with Bashiam provides her with a feeling of fulfillment which she has failed to achieve with her civilized husband. But Bashiam's is a wounded self that oscillates uneasily between tribal identity and British civility. Like Sindi Oberoi in Arun Joshi's novel *The Foreigner* (1968) and Billy Biswas in *The strange Case of Billy Biswas* (1971), Bashiam is left an alienated soul. He stands on the cross roads of the East and the West. Shyam M. Asnani rightly comments :

> Helen is thus presented to stand for the West's desire to understand the East and Bashiam with his obsession with the machine and technological progress, cut off from his traditional moorings, is supposed to represent the predicament of the modern youth of India (24).

Helen is particularly attracted towards the tribal men's hospitality and sincere affections which she misses in her Western company. In spite of their poverty and backwardness, she discovers peace and happiness in the Indian Tribal and Rural culture.

The novel ends with the death of the Tribal chief. As Helen and Mackendrick pay their last visit to the chief, he predicts that the rains will stop 'when the ridges rise clear' (22). They are always apprehensive of the safety of the tribal as Clinton is worried about the safety of the coffer dams. When it rains heavily, the watchman tries to comfort the Sahib's troubled mind telling him, "Do not worry, Sahib. The dams are strong and will hold." Clinton expresses his eagerness for termination of his burden. He says "only one has no wish to extend one's stay in this country" (201). This reveals Clinton's mood of restlessness and disgust as he contemplates to leave the country. But in contrast his wife takes farewell from the tribals, especially the wounded Bashiam, with cordiality and comforting words. The death of the chief symbolizes the end of old tradition and the emergence of the machine. But the novel ends with an ambivalent note that implies that, as Menon and Rao suggest :

> Merely mechanical progress cannot be the end of Human existence. The values of relationship, and the question of integrity and communication that enters into them cannot be sacrificed to iron and steel. This, in a nutshell, is Markandaya's concern in *The Coffer Dams* (169).

In *Two Virgins* Kamala Markandaya depicts the clash of values between traditional village life and westernized modern city life. She shows the impact of westernisation on the younger generation, specially the rural poor. The village is situated in the South of the Ganges and North of the Cauvery. Appa and Amma are typical South Indian names for parents. The novel studies the growth and development of two growing sisters, Lalitha and Saroja in a closely knit impoverished rural family, from innocence and ignorance to experience and wisdom.

It is through Saroja, the younger sister, that Markandaya narrates about the village life, her parents' response to the changing situations in the post independence India, her elder sister's tragic loss of identity and her own reactions to various experiences in her life. The two girls have been potrayed in contrast to each other inspite of being born and brought up in the same family, environment and parental care.

Coming in contact with Western people, their culture and educational pattern, village girls start revolting against traditional ideas of spiritualism, home-bound life and ethical code of conduct. Lalitha, educated in public school, trained by Anglicized teacher Miss Mendoza, is easily attracted towards opportunities offered by the metropolis. She feels enchanted by the alluring proposal of Mr. Gupta, the film director from the city, to embark on a career of acting in films. Gupta, who represents the corrupt and vile forces of the city, exploits Lalitha's innocence. The village is not advanced enough to accept a fallen girl. Neither Gupta nor Miss Mendoza come forward to rescue her when she tries to commit suicide. Her family members try their best to save her from disaster and shameful existence. But she cannot reconcile herself to the rural set up and hence, finally, goes back to the city to be lost in its moral chaos. From her example Saroja learns to be cautious about the city people who are hedonistic and morally unscrupulous.

While unfolding the two virgins' growing awareness of life in all its complexity, Kamala Markandaya also portrays the predicament of the rural poor. The novel revolves round the family of Appa, a freedom fighter, who has been appointed as a family planning advisor and is given an acre of land. Appa, Amma, their children and a dependant widow Aunt Alamelu constitute a lower middle class family in a South Indian village. Among the working class people in the village are Manikkam, the humble cultivator and the milkman, Chingleput, the sweet seller, Kannan, the unskilled carpenter and the blacksmith. These lowly placed ones lead an humble life. Manikkam's one-roomed hut is constructed of thatch, mud and inflammable bricks. Once the children upset his lamp which set the house on fire. He took four months to rebuild it. Hence, from that day he becomes cautious and panic stricken on Diwali celebrations. His poverty is due to his large family. The villagers' ignorance of family welfare measures cause poverty and suffering.

Lalitha gets disgusted with Aunt Alamelu who imposes restrictions on her movements. She is not allowed to celebrate Diwali with boys in a grand manner. When her aspirations to go to the city are bleak she curses 'The one-horse town, this backward place, this outpost of civilization' (84). She is aggrieved by the unfair attitude of sexual discrimination. Saroja feels sorry for the poor villagers eating grass and unedibles during the famine that broke out during the British regime. But what amazes her is the wide chasm between the rich and the poor existing even after Independence. Lalitha feels dejected at their poor stature. She cries, 'it is barbaric, not having a fridge.' She is convinced that fridge is not a luxury which the city people and the rich men possess but it is 'a necessity in a tropical country' (26). Saroja feels exasperated when she observes the village women collecting their daily need of water with much hardship. They have to go to the communal well and draw water by the pulley. The farmers' wives use the well, but the landowners who live in big houses have their own piped water. When manikkam's baby son contracts small pox, his wife prays god to save her son in exchange of a silver bangle. The baby dies being deprived of vaccination and proper medical care. Saroja is bewildered when Lalitha speaks to her about the costly donations like silver and gold the rich people contribute to the church. Tins, bottles, bits of broken mud pots, wheels, chains and all the dirt of the village are thrown into river polluting its water which is also used for drinking, cooking and cleaning purposes. The novel is replete with the description of the miserable conditions of Indian villages. The novel also depicts the travails that accompany transition from a rural, agrarian lifestyle to an urban, industrial way of life. The ageless rural civilization has been immensely affected by the insurgence of mechanization. There is a noticeable apprehension among the village workers. The blacksmith, the weavers, even Chingleput have the fear of machines usurping them.

Two Virgins is also a study in the contrasting attitudes among the older and the younger generations towards modern living and life style. As A.V. Krishna Rao comments, "Parents and aunt in varying degrees stand for the stability and continuity of the tradition of their village community while Mr. Gupta symbolizes the fast changing, superficial and immoral exploiting system of the city" (Continuity 21). The boys leave their native place for the city as there is nothing in the village to engage them. Aunt Alamelu is frightened and enraged when she learns that Lalitha is going to the city to join cinema and perform dances. She abhors the idea of her niece turning into a notch girl, while Lalitha explains that being an actress is an honourable profession in modern times. R.M. Varma studies this aspect of the novel and comments :

> *Two Virgins* shows great concern about the irresistible encroachment of new and material values borrowed from the west, on the ancient Indian beliefs and old established relationships within the family and the village (33).

In *Two Virgins,* Kamala Markandaya attempts at a study of the basic problem of the adolescent girls in modern India seeking an escape from the world of strict adult supervision, from the rural boundary into a wider world of wealth, glamour and pleasure. While Lalitha is irredeemably lost in the faceless crowd of the metropolitan world, Saroja gains wisdom from her sister's downfall. She undergoes a process of self-education being guided by the tradition bound Aunt Alamelu, the experienced Manikkam's wife and her sympathetic companion Chingleput. Thus Saroja is portrayed not only as the key figure who surveys the whole action of the novel, but also as a symbolic point of reconciliation between tradition and modernity.

As in *The Coffer Dams* Kamala Markandaya presents the slow and steady encroachment of Western technology in the Indian backward regions in her last novel *Pleasure City* published thirteen years after the publication of *The Coffer Dams.* The novel focuses on the problems of a struggling fishing community, as the

International Development Corporation from England undertakes a project of building a holiday resort named "Shalimar" in an unnamed fictional city in the remote coastal region of western India. In both the projects, the building of a Coffer dam and of a tourist resort, the British and the Indian Officers are employers of the poor workers. The Indian Labourers have been described as half-necked, underfed, untrained and uncivilized. Like the tribals, the fishermen are also tempted by offers of job with low wages. They have no organization, no disciplined method to put forth their grievances before their employers. The affluent managers and officers always look down upon the poor labourers.

There is a display of the luxurious living style of the British officers in palatial buildings and the poor workers' humble abode of huts. Yet their mutual cooperation and good understanding have been highlighted. Rikki, the fisher boy, who is an orphan from the age of five, is taken care of by another fisherman family. He is blessed with loving foster-parents as well as a friendly brother Muthu and a sweet sister Valli. As Rikki is young he is spared from fishing. He goes to Mrs. Bridie's school and learns English. But Muthu and other older boys are bound to go to the sea to catch fish and assist their parents in earning their livelihood. Mrs. Bridie is quite compassionate towards these young students who are irregular in school, for she knows that fishing is their way of life, and their means of livelihood. When Rikki is sixteen years old he accompanies Muthu to help the family. In good seasons and favourable weather they eat well but when fishing is out of season, they starve and run into debt.

The AIDCROP, a multinational corporation, is directed by the English Director Copeland Tully whose grandfather was once a part of the imperial regime. Tully lives in a luxurious dwelling place especially renovated for his stay. Like the establishment of tannery bringing urban ways of living to the village of Rukmani and Nathan, the luxury holiday resort causes perceptible change in the undeveloped stretch of the coastline. The natives who had no notion of the grandeur of the Empire, now observe with awe the advent of important looking men and women with shoes and spectacles in motor cars, setting tents in the coconut groves.

The novel presents a clear contrast between the conditions of the intruders and of the natives. Rikki is overburdened with the debt his father has incurred for the making of a boat. The money lender makes his life miserable by pressing upon him to repay the loan. Tully is surprised to learn from Rikki that at such tender age, a boy is in huge debt. Like Nathan's sons who leave behind their ancestral job of farming and go to distant tea plantation and factories for jobs, the young fishermen with no food at home and heavy load of debt join the Shalimar construction works. With the intrusion of the city men, prices of essential commodities shoot up. Rikki goes to the Shalimar where Tully gets impressed at his diligence and sincerity. He speaks English fluently. Tully assigns him the job of making a boat for the project director. Soon he is appointed as a life saver at Shalimar. During leisure time he lays mosaic at Avalon. Thus, he earns a good sum with his new assignment. He proves himself responsible and efficient when he rescues Corinna, Tully's wife from being drowned. He is quite contented with his new role as a waiter in Shalimar. He purchases a quartz watch, cloth for his mother. Tully offers him a shirt to wear to attend the celebrations on the day of 'Ministers' visit. Ramesh Chadha, pointing out the symbolic portrait of Rikki comments :

> Rikki representing a tribal origin, a section of Indian society living on the fringes of sustenance — open to natural hazards, himself becomes an emblem of the elemental forces of nature to be adopted and tamed by whosoever wishes. He is also representative of the pristine, idyllic life of primordial nature in sharp contrast with life in the materialistically advanced, sophisticated West (59.1990).

In spite of the racial and class differences, Tully and Rikky are drawn towards each other. Tully has made a yacht and knowing Rikki's fondness for the boat offers it to him as a parting gift when he leaves for England on completion of the project work. But to his utter amazement, he finds Rikki, the child of the sea, unwilling to return to nature. With the transition of time, the inevitable change in him has occurred. "He had gone forward, from mangy hut to school house, to Shalimar when it blossomed, moved on to Avalon, its grave, rich heights" (336).

Once Rikki has advanced from the old parental profession of fishing, he cannot take a backward step. After long years of experience of driving coach, building boats, and doing domestic works for the Britishers, he cannot adjust himself mentally to a return to the forsaken fishing life. He is now determined to work in Shalimar, not in the sea. Tully ruminates over the great loss the modern urban, technical civilization has brought to the innocent, and hardworking coastal people. He reflects, "This was a bought boy, sold on Shalimar, wherever he might pasture, his soul" (337).

Markandaya's perception of the poor and the downtrodden is thus informed by an ironic attitude that reflects a brooding sense of loss and pathos at the fast erosion of traditional values and human warmth in relationships as well as corrosion of human values at the cost of material aspirations and acquisitions. While the Indian poor have learnt to survive through centuries, in terms of their humanness, this is threatened by their forced entry into the new world of machines and machinations.

III

Kamala Markandaya's ironic attitude is further reinforced and is perhaps sharper when it comes to her observations on the Indian middle class. The middle class is neither poor nor rich, and thus while it deliberately distorts the 'human face,' it is yet unable to cope with the stress and pain that accompany the aspiration to move upward in social hierarchy.

In *A Silence of Desire* Kamala Markandaya demonstrates the strong impact of western culture and education on the mind of the middle class Indians. The complexity of human relationships has been examined from the point of view of ideological adjustment of an urban middle class couple. As A.V. Krishna Rao suggests :

> In her third novel *A Silence of Desire* (1960) Markandaya's diagrammatical representation of the contemporary consciousness shows up a new dimension of sensibility in that the fictional focus is on the psychological adjustment of an urban middle class family (Continuity, 47).

Dandekar, the protagonist of the novel, is a city dweller working as a clerk in a government department. His contact with the Europeans has given him a pragmatic and scientific outlook on life. This attitude is also shared by his colleagues in the office. Joseph believes in free love, while Ghosh, the senior officer follows the Western style of living and comments derogatively on Indian saints. Sarojini, Dandekar's wife, is a quiet, traditional Hindu housewife who is devoted to her domestic duties, taking care of her husband and children. But their peaceful and contented domestic life is threatened by the appearance of a spiritual leader, revered as the Swamy. Sarojini frequently visits him with the hope that the Swamy can heal her tumor while Dandekar insists on treatment in the hospital. This conflict gradually strains their conjugal relations. Rekha Jha says; 'His middle class living goes hand in hand with his middle class predicament rooted in traditional social pattern and culture, yet willing it away' (95).

Dandekar is torn between his love for his wife and his unfounded fear of the Swamy's control over her. There is a sarcastic note in the statement, 'He loved his wife; he was grateful to her, he was a fool and worse to have doubted her' (47-48). Even after fifteen years of marriage the couple lack a sense of adjustment and mutual tolerance. Like the Swamy in *Possession* who stands as a rival to Caroline in winning over the prodigious artist Val, Dandekar finds the Swamy as his adversary. The conflict in *possession* is mostly on aesthetic and materialistic level, whereas in *A Silence of Desire*, it is domestic and spiritual conflict that drifts them apart. Dandekar becomes suspicious and jealous of his wife because of a lack of communication between the two. Dandekar's educated mind cannot submit itself to the superstitious notions of his credulous wife. He suffers from a severe mental crisis when he finds her committed to faith healing. His unfounded suspicion about her relationship with the Swamy destroys his peace of mind both at home and in the office.

The portrait of Dandekar is one of the middle class working man who desires that his small earning is not recklessly spent. He is shocked when he comes to learn that Sarojini has given away the small store of silver cups, and gold chains they had saved for their daughter's marriage. He wants the articles to be deposited back, because he is not a rich man, he has no black money, he is not a blackmarketeer or a hoarder. Hence, when he meets the Swamy, he argues, 'We are not rich people, we cannot afford to give away so much' (155). He is sadly aware of the limitations of his middle class status, 'We're not rich, we never have been, we never will be' (157). Gradually, he grows intolerant and impatient as he feels neglected, his children uncared for and his wife frenzied. He resolves to settle the matter with his wife. With the help of the officers and his colleagues he succeeds in driving the Swamy out of their town. Inspite of this achievement, he is tormented by a sense of moral degradation and defeat when he realizes that Sarojini's surgical operation is firmly approved by the holy man. Hence he admits, 'He has done what I could not do. So I am to be humbled' (218). Thus, Dandekar is finally relieved of his mental tension, his suspicions being cleared. He feels tremendously belittled when he gets his 'treasured possessions' — 'the silver cups, the water-lily ash-tray and the chain from his son's neck' (224). He feels agonized at the deserted sight of the hermitage in the Swamy's absence.

Kamala Markandaya has fittingly selected the title of the novel from Longfellow's sonnet, '*The Three Silences of Molinos*' which opens with the following lines :

> Three silences there are; the first of speech,
> The second of desire, the third of thought.

In fact, the content of the novel corresponds more to the silence of speech as there is no mutual understanding between husband and wife. Lack of communication between the two wrecks peace at home. Dandekar's infatuousness, his carnal desires and his desire to keep his wife under his control turn him blind and unreasonable. K.S.N. Rao explains the breakdown of the family tie :

> Inner peace comes from a silence of all the three — speech, desire and thought — and this novel we see that the silence of speech in the wife is disturbed by Dandekar with his own desires, which he should have silenced at last for some time, and this disturbance leads to the loss of peace and harmony, the tranquility that he wants, so much when he sees the Banyan Tree (Silence, 350).

Like Dandekar, Sarojini also keeps things secret from her husband. She apprehends that he might not allow her to go to the swamy to be healed. Hence she argues with strong conviction, "You would have reasoned with me until I lost my faith because faith and reason do not go together, and without faith, I shall not be healed" (87). Sarojini is neither rich nor poor, neither highly educated nor illiterate, neither from a sophisticated society nor from a rural agrarian class. Her views are based on a middle-class disposition of quiet acceptance. She complains to her husband, 'You with your western notions, your superior talk of ignorance and superstition when all it means is that you do not know what lies beyond reason and you prefer not to find it out' (87).

Dandekar has never given a serious thought to his wife's problems, though he admits that she is the key figure in the family. His first mistake is not to enquire about her illness. When he tries to speak to her, 'Speech seemed locked somewhere beyond his dry lips, his constricted throat' (85). He is not satisfied with her explanations for staying away from home and taking refuge in a hermitage. When middle class people cannot fulfil their cherished desires they surrender themselves to a spiritual guide not for spiritual enlightenment but for relief from tensions. Margaret P. Joseph rightly observes :

> The theme is the clash between faith and reason and it provides the immediacy of a contemporary problem in India, but the real achievement of the author lies in the projection of this theme through awakening of a mind developing from thoughtless complacency to tremulous introspection (36).

Dandekar represents the typical middle-class householder who cannot afford any luxurious living. He usually walks to and from the office, saving his bus fare of six rupees with which he can manage to buy rose water, bangles, toilet articles for his wife, toys for the baby and trinkets for the girls and some sweetmeat. He considers even these as semi luxuries. If he works late at night in the office, he is not in a position to inform his wife because 'only officers can afford luxuries like telephone, a call to make sure the servants bring up your meal piping hot' (60).

This consciousness of class disparity always hurts him bitterly although Sarojini quite devotedly waits for him and serves him hot meal on his return from office.

Like Prem in Ruth Prawar Jhabvala's novel *The Householder*, Dandekar is tied to his routined and mechanical life in the city :

> His worries over children's illnesses, the intractability of servants, relatives in sufferableness, he usually forgot in office routine, or they were diminished in the greater woes of his colleagues. Or, if he had suffered harshness or injustice in the office, Sarojini's indignation, the extra comfort with which she took care to surround him, soon put things in their proper perspective (63).

Dandekar maintains a balance between the two worlds — his office and his home. Sarojhini blames him for his suspicions grounded on his colleagues' gossip. She says, 'You listened to every poisonous word of every petty clerk in your office and you believed it' (86). She is convinced that if she is treated in the hospital she would die the way her mother died after surgical operation. Dandekar has never tried to realize his wife's sentiments. He suffers mentally for his ego, adamancy and hypocrisy.

Dandekar has been placed in the middle section of the society. He is found taking pity on the street beggars who pour blessings if small coins are thrown at them. He is at least in a better position than the sickly, the destitute, the homeless, the beggars, the hungry and the starving millions. The clerks and other government officials of low rank are placed in between the affluent and the underfed. With his small income to feed his family, he cannot tolerate his valuables being donated to the Swamy but in the end he realizes that the Swamy may be a menace to the educated few, but is certainly a solace to the anguished soul, the tensed mind for whom he is a spiritual guide and psychological anchorage. Thus, once Sarojini comes back to him being cured of her physical ailments and superstitious notions, he regains the priceless possession of his life. The causes of domestic disharmony are removed and they revive once again their sweet music of life. Usha Pathania comments :

> The peace and happiness of the Dandekar family is restored. The unhappy interlude is over and the good old days return with the encouraging change that Sarojini and Dandekar have now achieved interpersonal fusion on both the places-physical as well as mental. A sort of compromise has been struck between scientific views of Dandekar and religious belief of Sarojini, the ties between them are stronger than before (95).

Two Virgins attempts to probe into the mental and psychological states of two young girls of middle class upbringing. Lalitha is born in a typical middle class family of Appa and Amma. Appa encourages her to utilize the first opportunity at her disposal to develop her artistic talent. She leaves her restricted village life and moves into the promising city life. She feels that her future career may be crushed under the communal weight of the outdated social systems. Through her experiences the author projects the emergence of new values, new social codes, cultural practices and life styles.

As Saroja grows, she observes her sister emerging from her rural middle class background and transcending her limitations of rusticity and social barriers. She joins the film industry in the city but becomes unsuccessful in her ambition to uplift her social position. Finally, Lalitha becomes rootless, losing her family affections as well as her moral life to the immoral industrialist Gupta. Now she fits herself neither to the rural community nor to the newly accepted urban surrounding in the same way as Beatie Bryant experiences. Arnold Wesker, the champion of working class, depicts in his play *Roots* (1959) the dilemma of an educated girl Beautie who, coming out of a rural and peasant background, struggles against social stigma. She is unsuccessful in bringing change to her basic traditional pattern at home and also in adopting herself to the sophisticated society she has been closely associated with. Lalitha like Beatie has been portrayed as a rebel against the existing social conventions which tend to resist any change and advancement that the youth aspires.

The theme of rootlessness, alienation and loss of identity is more seriously treated in *The Nowhere Man* Srinivas belongs to an Indian upper middle class family, in possession of landed property, forest plants and an extended house which accommodates four generations of family members. Under political pressure during the time of national upheaval when he emigrates to London with his newly wed wife Vasantha, he dreams of a happy and contended life. Vasantha aspires to live in their newly purchased three-storey building with her sons. But soon misfortunes follow one after another. His younger son Seshu dies in war, his wife Vasantha dies of consumption and the elder son Laxman stays away from home. Contrary to the middle class Indian parents' expectations, Laxman marries an English girl without parental consent. He stays in Plymouth in his own flat. The parents are not allowed to share joys and comforts with their grand children. Their usefulness is no longer recognized. Srinivas, the widower, is left to the National Health Care. In his sixties, he suffers from leprosy and thus he is condemned to social alienation. The tender care of the middle aged English divorcee Mrs. Pickering sustains and comforts Srinivas in his later life of suffering.

The middle class in the post-war Britain suffer due to economic instability and unemployment. Fred. Mike, joe and Bill represent the frustrated youth who react violently against the Indian emigrants like Srinivas. In searth of a decent job Frederick Fletcher, the son of Srinivas' neighbour, moves to Australia but is not satisfied there with the job of a road mender. He is not a skilled practitioner, hence he comes back to his country where to his utter disgust he finds the emigrants prospering on his land. He complains, 'They came in hordes. Occupied all the houses, filled up the hospital beds and their off spring took all the places in schools' (163). In spite of his mother's advice to treat the neighbours humanly like a true Christian, Fred goes on nourishing his hatred for the expatriates. He target is Srinivas, who on migrating from India thrives in business and gradually occupies a multi-storeyed building in London. Because of his colour and race he is condemned and threatened, 'You got no right to be living in this country' (164). Srinivas' friend Abdul of Zanzibari once warns him about the Britishers' antagonistic attitude. He is surprised at such intolerant attitude towards one who has turned into a septuagenarian and has been a British citizen since long.

Like Anita Desai's tragic hero Baumgartner in her novel *Baumgartner's Bombay* Srinivas feels insecure in the country he has lived for fifty years. Like Baumgartner who gets warmth and friendship in some Indians like Habibuyllah and Chimandal in his business activities, Srinivas also gets company and nursing from Mrs. Pickering and Dr. Radcliffe, a kindred soul helping the diseased and the destitute. Both the expatriates are lonely, suffering old men killed brutally in the end. Dr. Radcliffe is terribly shocked by the dogma of racial hatred leading to the brutal action of killing an innocent old man. He says, 'He is dead and we have all had a hand in it' (298). Mrs. Pickering is also aggrieved at this degeneration of human relationships. She finds similarity between the killing of Srinivas and the action of Abel when he kills his brother Cain. Dieter Riemenschneider reflects, 'Man's alienation from himself because of the system he is to live with can hardly be felt more painfully by him as when he turns against himself and becomes ashamed of his human feelings' (141-142). This inhuman act is vindicated by the accidental death of Fred who is himself killed by the fire he has set to kill the innocent Srinivas.

The Indian middle class, as is evident in Kamala Markandaya's novels, is torn between the two irreconcilable worlds of traditional moral and religious order on the one hand, and on the other, the emerging order of a utilitarian and materialistic society. The middle class India sometimes tries to strike a compromise, but more often tends to be lured by the new temptations of money and pleasure. But whatever the choice, the middle class mind remains essentially ambivalent in his attitude to life and living.

IV

While the poor and the middle classes in India are crushed by the colonial mindset of subservience and stoic acceptance of suffering, the upper class in India perpetuates this feudal subversion through control of social power. There are, of course, a few illustrious exceptions who are compassionate and loving, who look at their own class as highly alienated and socially aggressive. Markandaya's fictional world reflects both the subversive and the rebellious factions of the rich and upper class in both the colonial and post-colonial India.

In her second novel *Some Inner Fury*, Kamala Markandaya has studied the mode of living of an affluent society in the background of the political upsurge of 1942. During this time the struggle for independence of the country had reached a decisive stage. Unlike Rukmani, Nalini or Sarojini, the narrator heroine, Mira, belongs to the upper class. The story of romance of Mira and Richard has been subordinated to the narrative of nationalistic movement which dominates the life of people during the thirties and the forties.

Mira, the youngest member of an aristocratic and Westernized family has been brought up with all urban sophistication. She is well aware of her superior status, which is evident from what she thinks of her family :

> My mother went to play bridge and to keep my father company. I went because I was taken, and to learn; to mix with Europeans. This last part of my training, for one day soon I would marry a man of my own class, who like my brother, would have been educated abroad, and who would expect his wife to move as freely in European circles as he himself did (24).

Mira is happy that the club provides amenities such as billiard room, squash court and tennis court. They have two dining halls, two sets of cooks, one western and the other Indian. Women go to the club and speak English to the English visitors. They serve liquor while entertaining their English guests. Such aristocratic life style with glamour of the well-to-do and opportunities of plentitude build up her back ground during her adolescence.

Mira's brother Kitsamy is educated in Oxford. Being Western oriented he does not find anything valuable in Indian culture. During the British rule such anglicized men from among the upper class enjoyed high posts in Government services. Kit qualifies himself as a Civil Servant and holds the prestigious and powerful post of District Magistrate. His Westernized outlook alienates him from his own countrymen. Amidst plenty and prosperity he looks down upon the poor people. He marries Premala, a girl with traditional Indian attitudes. Like Kamala in B. Rajan's *The Dark Dancer* (1959) and Kusum in Nayantara Sahgal's *A Time to be Happy* (1958) Premala promotes humanitarian feelings in her community. She enjoys her-selfless service while Kit keeps himself aloof from his countrymen. Premala engages her self in educating the poor, illiterate and unprivileged ones. The English Missionary Hickey has established a school for children. Premala feels elated in the company of the innocent young children. She rather feels suffocated in Kit's sophisticated artificial life style. Kit's English friend Richard Marlowe has got a job as Governor's military aide in India. While Kit has aversion for the common men, Richard is quite compassionate towards the poor. Unlike some English officers in India, he shows no bias, indifference or any sense of racial superiority. He even borrows Indian garments such as shirt, dhoti and chappals from the servants. It is, ironically, Mira's father who looks contemptuously at the poor workers, and blames Richard, 'The Englishman has a lot to learn, I do not think his countrymen will approve his unconventionality' (14).

Mira enjoys Richard's simplicity and goodness when he sits on the floor in the company of the villagers. Both of them have a feeling of 'warmth and understanding' (135) when they make their survey of villages under their plan. They spend six weeks in the exclusive company of each other in their South India tour. Despite her mother's objections Mira carries on her close relationship with Richard. With all the apparent life style of the upper class, paradoxically, Mira's mother cannot easily accept Westernized behaviours of her daughter. She feels quite uneasy at the close relationship of a grown-up girl with an Englishman. Richard, a well-paid British official, feels shocked at the living conditions of the Indians. Rich and affluent as they are, Richard and Mira are appalled at the agony of the starving poor.

In Roshan, Kamala Markandaya has portrayed the figure of a liberated woman with clear conscience and universal outlook. She is born in one world and educated in another. She is capable of moving in both with ease and efficiency. She, in fact, belongs to the majority of Indian national leaders who forsake their happy family life and comfortable luxurious living to take active part in the political struggle against colonial rule. K.S. Venkatramani in his political novel *Kandan the Patriot* (1932) has portrayed such emerging liberated women freedom-fighters like Rajeshwari who renounces the comforts of her domestic life to dedicate herself to the national cause. Roshan, the journalist, runs a progressive newspaper to apprise the public of the various constructive works the nationalists have undertaken. She engages Mira in her establishment. Mira is asked to report on a peasant resettlement in the neighborhood. But while on work, coming in close contact with the villagers and their problems, she realizes that 'it is no easy matter to construct, as it were overnight, a complete village; for villages cannot be rushed into life like towns' (137).

Govind, the adopted brother of Mira and Kit, hates the high class society and rejects the offer of any clerical job to him in his foster father's business. He decides to engage himself in some respectable patriotic activities, or as he puts it, 'community works.' In contrast to Kit, Govind likes to be educated in his own country. Mira remembers the scene on the day Kit returns home getting educated in England :

> ...so many of us gathered there on that narrow station platform-parents, aunts, uncles, friends, all of us carrying garlands in welcome, and beyond, in a beaming semi circle, the servants laden with bunches of plantains and amphora of rose waters and still beyond officious peons, green-belted, brass-buckled, hustling aside onlookers and travellers alike that this public platform might be ours alone (8).

In contrast to such idolization of the West, Govind likes the old Indian tradition and values and is extremely critical of the British way of life. He joins the nationalist movement and fights against the British rule. His extreme and violent acts lead to Premala's accidental and sudden tragic end. Hickey, the founder of the school, is terribly upset to see his life's work destroyed in fire. The Britishers get alarmed at the inner fury of the unruly, violent crowd. Richard and Mira become conscious of the futility of their attachment when stones are thrown at them. Mira's personal remark distinguishing 'my people' from 'your people' (138) is significant in the perspective of the tense political situation. Margaret P. Joseph reflects on such breakdown of personal relationship :

> The volcanic 'inner fury' of the nation crept destroying the illusion of harmony, with wide connotations of relationships between races and nations. The microcosm of individual relationship is also destroyed by the inner fury of love, jealousy and violence (25-26).

From her bitter experience Mira learns that during a national upheaval, there is inevitably a psychological barrier between the ruler and the ruled. Hence, altering her course, she renounces wealth, honour and even love in order to identify herself with the Indian sentiments. This suggests that inter-racial emotional bond can be threatened by the powerful pressures of political exigencies. Once Nathan is uprooted from the land, he loses his identity but Rukmani survives all hazards of life and finally returns to the native place in a calm and serene mood. Premala dies in a mob fury as she cannot adjust her idealism to the irrational demands of her Westernized husband. Samares C. Sanyal rightly observes :

> The delineation of the roots of different classes of Indian society is Kamala Markandaya's continuing theme. She has artistic insight enough to know where the roots are and how do the roots get disentangled resulting in inter-cultural tension and changing individuals. Her chief merit lies in that she presents the direct and indirect clashes between two sets of values in Indian ways of life without authorial commentary (94).

In spite of the tragic separation of Mira and Richard, *Some Inner Fury* ends with a note of patriotism as Mira sacrifices her personal pleasures for the sake of a greater national cause. She joins the mob defending Govind against the false allegation of murdering Kit. There is a quest for self-discovery. When she makes her final decision to depart from Richard and join the crowd of demonstrators, she has certainly realized her roots. Her wounded self is discernible when the external fury of the crowd demanding Govind's release suppresses her emotional inner fury. As a grown up girl she is to decide her course of action. She prepares herself to embrace the fire of revolution finally realizing that 'the forces that pulled us apart were too strong' (285). Punim Juneja rightly observes :

> *Some Inner Fury* reiterates the fact that a meeting of East and West is always possible at the level of personal relationships. But by placing Mira and Richard in a particular historical context, Kamala Markandaya shows how sometimes social and political compulsions become too strong to be withstood and one is compelled to take sides (185).

Kamala Markandaya's most ambitious and mature work *The Golden Honeycomb* reveals her keen awareness of the colonial history centered round kings and princes. The majestic life of the kings and princes has become a major concern of some of the eminent Indian English novelists. Mulk Raj Anand, the champion of the down-trodden, has portrayed in *Private life of an Indian Prince (1953)*, the life of the prices who impress the British Government by their loyalty and submission to British sovereignty. The story narrated by Dr. Shankar describes the common life of an Indian Maharaja, Victor Edward George Ashok, whose political power declines on account of his obsessive passion for Ganga Devi, his power-loving paramour. He develops mental derangement that leads to a disastrous end. Anand delineates the moral and political corruption of the native rulers of the Indian states with sharp irony and sarcasm.

Manohar Malgonkar's *The princes* (1963) narrates the political fate of a small princely state Begwad which is amalgamated into the Indian union after 1947. As in Anand's novel, Malgonkar's focus of attention is on the private life of the princes, the decline of princely power and the psychological problems of the princes. Both the Maharaja and his son Abhaya raj, the narrator of the story, are vindictive, violent, sensual, passionate and doomed. However, tortured and disgraced the subjects and revolutionaries like Kanak chand may be, the awakening of nationalism and democratic idealism does hold the promise of political freedom. Abhaya, the young prince of the days of enlightenment becomes aware of the loss of sovereignty of the State. The author sarcastically points out how after Independence the bureaucrats and the politicians turn liars, corrupt, hypocrites and sycophants. Gandhi's idealism is soon forgotten and lost. The old Maharaja prefers to be killed by a ferocious tiger rather than being harassed by leaders wielding crude political power. He courts his tragic death realizing the inevitable end of the princely powers, honours and privileges.

Like Anand and Malgonkar who have exhibited the decline and fall of the age-old institution of monarchy, Kamala Markandaya in her longest and only historical novel *The Golden Honeycomb* dramatizes the vicissitudes of three generations of the princely family of Devapur covering a period of about a century from 1850 to 1950. She has adroitly managed to turn the story into a saga of patriotism as well as the growth of individual consciousness and national awareness. Like the other two novels, *The Golden Honeycomb* describes not only the glittering ceremonies, pageantries, rituals, splendorous festivals, banquets, colourful dresses and jewellery associated with princely societies, but also the tensions and compulsions of kings and princes in an atmosphere of imperialistic pressures and nationalist movements.

Bawajiraj I, the King of Devapur State, is imprisoned for his spirit of Independence leaving the throne vacant. The political Agent, the British Resident and the Dewan, a Brahmin Chief Minister, select a Young man of eighteen as the King. Though this young man does not belong to the Kshatriya caste which holds the exclusive and hereditary right to rule a princely state, he is christened as Bawajiraj-II, the Maharaja of Devapur. This act of the British is a gross contravention of Indian social system where caste determines the class. Bawajiraj II being elevated to the higher caste of the ruling class ascends the throne and remains loyal and devoted to the British Government, who 'have early understood the importance of the Native Princes, the one class in the country bound to them by every tie of self-interest, in the Imperial scheme. They are concerned to devise buffers which will protect them against the wrath of the masses and to ensure the emergence of Maharajahs amenable to their purpose' (33).

Bawajiraj II innocently 'takes pleasure in his new riches and privileges, in the manner of his elevation which is arranged with pomp and circumstance' (10). He is vainglorious in his show of pomposity and royal gesture of feeding hundreds of beggars but in reality he is like to puppet in the hands of the Britishers. The dynasty he founds is 'consecrated by the British presence before it can achieve its full potential' (13).

Bawajiraj II meets his death prematurely in an accident of horse riding. His son succeeds him to the throne as Bawajiraj III under the guardianship of the mother Dowager Maharani and the British Resident Arthur Copeland. Even though the young prince has been trained in European system of education at the cost of the poor and needy natives, he feels humbled as 'most of the ruling that matters has been taken from his hands' (39). He marries Shanta Devi who begets four daughters. But the king is blessed with a son from his love with a commoner, Mohini who chooses to remain as a concubine and to bring up her son Rabindranath as heir to the throne. Because of Rabi, the heir to the throne, Mohini, though a commoner, enjoys the splendours of royal life. Both the widowed Maharani and her companion Mohini are compassionate towards the poor people. But Bawajiraj III is alienated from his people because of his western education and aristocratic life style.

Mohini engages an Indian Pandit as a tutor for her son Rabi, rather than send him to study in Chief's college or the Military Academy as did his father and grand father. Rabi is immensely inspired by the ancient tales of India. He travels with his mother, grandmother and the Pandit throughout the state and comes in close contact with the common men, women and their children. As Rabi grows, he develops friendship with Janaki, the sweeper's girl, Das, the gardener's son and Usha, the Dewan's daughter. Rabi's attachment with Sophie does not last long as her mother Lady Copeland cannot appreciate anything Indian. But Rabi and Usha march together towards the state of freedom. Rabi realizes that his royal responsibility must be directed towards the welfare of the people.

In his six month extensive journey Rabi gains knowledge of reality, the life beyond the palace and a fervent national spirit. Bearing the name of the great poet and nationalist Rabindranath Tagore, Rabi feels enlightened in close contact of nature. At the sight of the beautiful green paddy field he gets enthralled and excited but feels agitated when the Pandit informs him that the formers who grow the bumper harvest live from hand to mouth. He recognizes his father's false and superficial claims, 'My father says every one in his state is well-fed' (80). He feels sorry for the large gap existing between the palace and the Residency on the one hand and the subjects on the other. While the people in power enjoy all the privileges, the common man suffers under the hardship of famine and draught. While his father is elated at the news of his son being approved by the Viceroy as the heir to the throne of Devapur, Rabi feels unhappy as he is well aware of the status of the native states, 'a fragile golden honeycomb' (237). He promises to raise a voice of protest against the King who is callous towards the starving peasants. He is deeply moved by the Pandit's perception of poor people as 'walking skeletons' (103).

In the Great Delhi Durbar scene a remarkable change comes over Rabi. He is astounded and shocked to see the grand celebrations of the Viceroy's accession to the throne with a 'glare of jewels,' 'flow of silk,' 'glittering elegance' (156) and the imperial procession which diminishes his father's position as a native ruler. The reactions of the viewers have been narrated ironically and poignantly.

> The Indian view was necessarily divided between the elite and the proletariat. Spokesmen for the proletariat were, later on, apt to call it a vulgar extravaganza that affronted the impoverished nation. The proletariat, however, at least that portion of it perched on the earth mound outside the amphitheater thrown up especially for them-these lucky citizens from their grand stand view found it a thoroughly enjoyable spectacle. The elite, but for one or two carping dissenters, pronounced it an outstanding success (157).

There is a genial satire in the exposition of the simplicity, innocence and ignorance of the suffering multitude in a poor country in contrast to a few privileged ones. There is crude display of loyalty of the Kings and Princes to the British throne, admiration of soldiers and Bawajiraj III, and Rabi's awareness of the Pandit's indignation. A form of father-son conflict can also be discerned in Malgonkar's *The Princes*. Abhayaraj in his confrontation with his father, maharaja of Begwad, leads the princely kingdom to its destruction. Instead of presenting the Indian Army, Indian forest, old feudal system and lovely hills, Kamala Markandaya weaves her plot in terms of a humanistic stance. Bawajiraj III is totally inhuman. His weaknesses and excesses have been exposed. His oppressions of the subjects, indifference to their needs are pointed out as stark reality. With his glorious possessions of jewel chambers, tracts of fertile land, caskets of precious gems and fully equipped armies, Bawajiraj III is not at all disturbed at the draught, famine and flood that make people destitute. When the buoyant father is overjoyed at the arrangement of the Simla trip, the son broods over the poor men's problems. The Maharaja's wide circle of guests at lunch, dinner and picnic parties, his moonlight mystery excursions have actually no impact on the enlightened son who feels suffocated thinking of the turbulent areas. On their way to Bombay to fetch their Rolls-Royce cars they are stranded because of the agitation of the cotton mill workers and the dock workers. The agitated crowd shouts, throws stones and breaks glasses when the police disperses them. Rabi is wounded and is rescued by a mill worker, Jaya who treats and nurses him in her humble hut. It is from this experience that Rabi realizes the misery of the 'empty-belly race' (289) fighting for livelihood. Margaret P. Joseph rightly comments :

> The English and their counterparts, the rajas, have alienated themselves from the lives of the ordinary people of India, but the 'golden honeycomb' which has cocooned them from reality is now beginning to disintegrate as the aspirations of the common men are made known (91).

Rabi's acute perception of the struggle for existence emerges from his intimate relations with women — his grandmother, the Dowager, his mother Mohini and his friends Jaya, Janaki and Usha. His love for Sophie is not objected by Arthur Copeland Inspite of Lady Copeland's bitterness and distaste of the Indians.

When Copeland goes to England Mr. Buckridge remains in charge of Residency. He is responsible for levying salt tax on the poor inhabitants who resist it tooth and nail. Rabi is happy to see Copeland return and taking the charge of Residency from the cruel and unsympathetic Buckridge. Bawajiraj III is silent witness of the great change that is imminent and inevitable. With the blessing and encouragement of the Dowager Maharani Manjula and Mohini, the common people led by the spirited social workers, Rabi and Usha, eventually succeed in their mission. Rabi's soul is not wounded as Nathan's, Ira's, Mira's, Dandekar's, Valmiki's or Srinivas. He has tried his best to overcome impediments. In fact, in him is combined the best of the East and the best of the West. Coming across the varieties and richness of India, Rabi becomes dedicated to the causes of humanity and nationalism. Arthur Pollard remarks :

> It might even be said that Rabi's history is a progress to understanding and then to act in a movement that takes him from admiration of his father with unquestioning acceptance of the *status quo*, through the influence of his mother and his Pandit, to a rejection of his princely role and the assumption of the leadership of popular protest (30).

Rabi is the product of a new age dominated by the spirit of awakening and liberation. The feminine forces act strongly on his growing mind. His youthful vigour is most effectively directed towards affecting change of national destiny. The old order changes yielding place to new. The chronological and historical framework of the narration and fictional account of the events reflect the plight of a fading feudal order and embody a vision of an emerging social order based on the dignity of the individual.

V

Kamala Markandaya's fictional world is crowded by characters of every kind who represent a typical cross-section of India. These characters are destined to act, speak and think in particular ways determined by their social class. It is this class-consciousness which is at the root of fictional tension and moral polemics in the novels of Markandaya. Sensitive characters attempt to fight against destiny in the face of anguish and suffering, while most other characters, particularly women, choose to suffer their destiny in calm acceptance of pain and humiliation.

2

Gender Bias and Resistance

In recent years, there has been a plethora of theoretical speculations on the problems of woman in her feminine and female identities in the context of social and interpersonal relationships. Many Indian women novelists in English have reflected, in their writings, a sharp concern with the role and status of Indian women in terms of social and familial power. Kamala Markandaya's novels embody a profound and sensitive understanding of the feminine and the female in Indian ethos. Women in her novels fall into two distinct categories : (a) those who acquiesce their traditional social roles and perceive ideal womanhood in terms of being an obedient daughter, a subservient wife, a protective mother and only a marginal participant in decision making, (b) those who militate against the constraints of traditional Indian womanhood, who attempt to assert social and sexual power in the face of socio-moral resistance.

Kamala Markandaya's first book *Nectar in a Sieve* exposes the traditional attitude of the Indians towards a female child at her very birth. With the birth of her first born Ira, Rukmani with tears of disappointment exclaims, 'A girl's body-what woman wants a girl for her first born?' (19). She supports her husband's view that a male child is an asset and a girl child is a liability to the family. But ironically the couple cannot lead a happy and prosperous life even if five sons are born to them successively. Nathan thinks that educating the girl child is sheer waste. In fact, Rukmani's education cannot help her to earn for the destitute family. Ira marries with dowry of hundred rupees, the maximum that her parents could offer. Rukmani easily reconciles herself to Ira's ill fate when her husband, being accused of barrenness deserts her. But the irony is that in their abject poverty it is the daughter who helps the family financially. At least she can feed the starving Kuti who dies painfully, slowly for want of milk. Their sons are no longer symbols of hope. Both Rukmani and Nathan lament over the departure of their sons from the land to distant places and different occupations. Their last hope of survival is lost when they cannot trace their son Murugan in the unfriendly city.

Rukmani seems to conform to the traditional image of women embodied in the mythical figures of Sita and Savitri who silently bear all hardships and remain devoted to their husbands. Born of the village headman and married to a tenant farmer below her family status, her good soul speaks of her husband as one "who was poor in everything but in love and care for me" (8). She feels proud of him as he is efficient in farming, in maintaining the household single handedly and is a loving husband. Though the knowledge of Nathan's adultery with Kunti in his youth is agonizing, she hardly ever betrays her feelings of jealously and anguish. On the other hand, her faith and reliance on her husband remain unabated. She is the symbol of unimpeachable chastity and unswerving devotion.

Rukmani stands by Nathan in times of both happiness and suffering, during bumper harvest and draught. During their abject penury Nathan feels grateful to her and declares 'you are a good wife, …I would not have any other' (84). Together they suffer misfortunes — the loss of their beloved sons, land, home, humiliations in the town, the grievance of their daughter and final separation. Rukmani exhibits her tremendous power of tolerance and patience when she speaks her last words to the dying husband, "If I grieve, I said, it is not for you, but for myself beloved, for how shall I endure to live without you, who are my love and my life?" To Nathan's ironical question "Have we not been happy together?" she replies confidently, "Always, my dearest, always" (187). After losing her husband she returns home with the diseased city boy Puli and joins her son Selvam and daughter Ira with a renewed desire to survive. Rukmani is portrayed not only as a devoted wife, but also as a loving, caring and sensible mother, a loyal friend, a helping neighbour, a considerate mother-in-law and a model housewife. As an incumbent of the traditional Indian values of chastity, devotion and integrity, she is genuinely the true voice of endurance. C.T. Indra rightly comments on this close study of a woman's feelings and thoughts, her sufferings and struggle :

> Kamala Markandaya has managed to give full play to a woman's self cast in a relatively unadventurous social milieu..... she proves that within the traditional role she can accommodate her other roles as a human being (71).

The Savitri metaphor has been ironically used in R.K. Narayan's *The Dark Room* (1938). Savitri tries to break the mythical image by leaving her home when she can no more tolerate her husband Ramani's extramarital relations. She tries to commit suicide but is rescued by Mari whose wife Ponni advises her to assert her position in the family by handling domestic conflicts with iron hand. Eventually Sabitri returns home signifying the importance of the dark room for an Indian wife who cannot enjoy a life of liberation.

This traditional portrait of woman as Sita or Savitri has not changed even after independence. In *Where Shall We Go This Summer*? Anita Desai portrays Sita as a rebel against the conventional patterns of life. She is fatigued with the conventional image of a woman. She leaves the city and goes to her father's mansion in the village in search of peace and contentment but finally comes back home with her husband Raman for the future prospect of the children. Thus, Kamala Markandaya, R.K. Narayan and Anita Desai show how Rukmani, savitri and Sita represent Indian women struggling for their rightful position in the family which is denied to them in the unjust, harsh and indifferent society.

A Handful of Rice is the only novel of Kamala Markandaya which begins with love at first sight that eventually finds its fulfillment in marriage. It is the study of the ennobling effect of love of an attractive young woman on a vagabond, unsocial youngman who is subsequently converted into a loving husband

and a responsible householder. Ravi, like other unemployed youngmen of his native place migrates to the city to overcome poverty and hunger. But in the city he faces the same problem of meeting the basic need of food and shelter. In search of this he happens to join a group of hooligans led by Damodar. Apu, the city tailor takes pity on the starving youngman and offers him as job of apprentice in his shop. Ravi's romantic interest in Nalini, the second daughter of Apu, marks the first turning point in his life. He accepts the job gladly for the sake of Nalini :

> Nalini, his girl. He said it to himself sweetly, roundly, secretly and it filled him with a delicious sense of pleasure. Nalini the girl who could make a man feel like a man even outside the jungle of his choosing, the girl for whom he was ready to repudiate all in his life that was unworthy (33).

At the outset, with Nalini he settles down to happy domesticity. Like Nathan and Rukmani, this newly-wed couple lead a happy conjugal life. As is usual in a city, Ravi soon develops aspirations for greater physical and material comfort. Fed up with the congested living in Apu's house, he dreams of a big room, a bicycle to move and a comfortable bed to sleep on. Nalini entreats him not to feel envious of the affluent people, to be content with whatever they have. She argues, "They are a different class... Ordinary folk like us can never be like them" (75). This shows Nalini's sense of adjustment and pragmatism. In spite of being beaten and ill-treated by her husband in his drunkenness, she tries her best to bring his wayward husband to the right path. She dissuades him to be associated with the smugglers. When Ravi gets frustrated with non-materialization of his ever-spiraling dreams, Nalini acts as a strong and powerful stimulus in helping him withdraw from the gangsters' clutches.

It is a crucial period in Ravi's life when he faces the moral dilemma of vascillating between the watchful moral guidance of his wife and the miscreant Damodar's temptations for immense material prosperity. He is in a fix, whether to adopt Damodar's foul means or sustain on honest and hard labour demanded by his wife. Like Hamlet he procrastinates action since he is unable to resolve the tension between the material benefits in Damodar's methods and the moral responsibilities of a good citizen, between depravity and conscience. But finally he stands against "the shoddy morality of a hypocritical society" (217).

Ravi tries to change his financial situation after being rescued by Apu from Damodar's world of moral depravity. But he is soon disillusioned when, after Apu's death he cannot manage the household properly because of his inefficiency, tactlessness and poor dealings with customers. He is unable to meet the needs of his wife. He is shocked most when his son Raju dies. He now realizes that he would rather steal and be rich than beg in the name of self respect. His deep concern for Nalini induces him to rebel against social distinctions, but he contemplates, "Rebel, and a contract might be lost, the steady wage would be lost, and then what of Nalini? He had to think of her, he had to think of himself for that matter. There seemed to be no answer" (84).

Tortured by abject penury, Nalilni quietly leaves her husband after Raju's death and goes to her sister's place. Ravi realizes now that in a society which is so inconsiderate, honesty would mean nothing. He fights against the society represented by the European memsahibs, the policemen and the rice godowns. After the death of his son, he castigates society, calling it "Them, Society, Guilty of casual murder " (231). He feels frustrated when he sees no chance of success. As Margaret P. Joseph rightly assesses the situation, Ravi is "destroyed by a false society, represented by the 'People' who think he has no feelings, who give him no privacy, who pin him down, actually and metaphorically, who give orders, who have money. His harsh treatment of Nalini, his incest with his mother-in-law, are indirect results of this frustrated rage against society" (62-63). Whenever discouraged and tortured by the world, Ravi finds solace and happiness in his love for Nalini. Ultimately he rejects the path of violence and tries to maintain his integrity for the sake of Nalini. Ravi and Nalini finally emerge, amidst all the hazards of poor living, as intimate lovers who share each other's woes and joys.

Traditionally Indian women feel elated and fortunate enough to beget a son as their first born. Nalini feels herself supremely blessed when Raju is born. Her sister Thangam feels that she is unfortunate in not having a son. Apu is sorry to have two daughters and no son to assist him in his old age. In spite of such deep faith in male supremacy, mothers do not discriminate between sons and daughters when it comes to bringing them up or supporting them in their hours of crisis and suffering. Jayamma never allows Nalilni to go with Ravi alone. Ravi fondly remembers his sisters who were closely protected until their marriage. Mulk Raj Anand in *Untouchable* shows how a motherless girl Sohini becomes a victim of molestation. In *Two Leaves and a Bud,* Leila remains safe only as long as her mother is alive. Apu allows his daughters to stay with him even after their marriage. Similarly, Rukmani provides security and shelter to Ira when she is deserted by her in-laws. This security of the girls is threatened when there is a financial crisis. Ravi in abject poverty drives out Thangam's husband from his house. In an outrage he goes to the extent of beating his wife and ill-treating his mother-in-law Ira is tolerated even when she turns into a prostitute under extremely strained financial condition. In the traditional Indian society, moral depravity of the male is never questioned where as women always submit themselves to the desires and pleasures of men. Rukmani silently endures Nathan's extra-marital adventures in the interest of a peaceful marital life. As K.S. Narayan Rao remarks :

> Markandaya's novels deal with contemporary Indian society, which is a traditional society in state of flux and change, and reveal a spectrum of moral attitudes on the part of the characters that people the fictional world, which include the traditionally moral, the immoral and the amoral attitudes. Although her woman characters are never relegated to the background and are, in fact, better drawn than their male counterparts, it is usually the men who get away with their delinquent sexual conduct (love, 69-70).

Husband-wife relationship being the most intimate and complex of all relationships, the conflict between tradition and modernity finds itself projected in the Indian social custom of marriage. R.K. Narayan in his *The Guide* and Raja Rao in his *The Serpent and the Rope* deal with the theme of estrangement between husband and wife on grounds of temperamental incompatibility and attitudinal differences. The failure of the marriage of Ramaswamy and Madeleine, of Marco and Rosie is due to such marital discord caused by failure of understanding and communication.

Kamala Markandaya's *A Silence of Desire* is a psychological study of strained husband-wife relationship, based upon misunderstanding. It is the story of a typical middle-class Indian married couple, Dandekar, a Junior Clerk in a government department and Sarojini, a duty-bound and devoted wife. Gradually the domestic bondage gets threatened by lack of communication leading to suspicion on the fidelity of Sarojini. In their initial fifteen years of marriage they enjoy harmonious married life. Dandekar is full of praise for his wife. She is acknowledged as the loving mother, an ideal house-wife and a devoted spouse. As Dandekar admits, 'She was a good wife, Sarojini, good with the children, an excellent cook, an efficient manager of his household.....' (7).

The cordial relation of the couple does not last long as there is no frank discussion on any issue. Rather they oppose each other on various issues. Specially Sarojini's opinions are never cared for, her traditional beliefs are outright rejected. It is Dandekar's scientific and rational views that are imposed upon his wife. Sarojini's faith is founded upon Eastern mysticism. She worships Tulsi plant as an image of God. Such superstitious beliefs of a tradition-bound woman are viewed by a modernist husband with scepticism. The friction gets intensified when Dandekar observes his wife's frequent absence from home neglecting her domestic duties. But he cannot dare ask her about the photograph of the stranger he discovers in her box. Instead, he nurtures a suspicion in his mind about Sarojini's chastity. Usha Pathania aptly observes :

> Dandekar is a male chauvinist for whom the wife is like a robot or some sophisticated mechanized device for the fulfillment of his needs. He cares for her but shows a fleeting interest in her ideas, attitudes and thoughts (87).

Mutual trust and confidence is the backbone of an enduring emotional bond. Sarojini is afraid of her husband who would never believe her words, hence hides her illness. Dandekar has no guts to ask her directly where she goes regularly. Such communication gap drifts them apart and poisons their mind.

When she releases the news about her attempt at faith-cure, Dandekar opens his heart to her, 'I was mad,' he said, 'I went mad because I loved her. Is that a crime? Is it possible to love without jealousy?' (87).

Dandekar has no spiritual moorings to sustain him in his desperation. He soon realizes his mistake of neglecting his wife and his home. When he discovers that his wife is getting dissociated from him and is driven towards her spiritual guide, the Swamy, he is disillusioned and then frantically searches for a way to rescue himself and his wife from the turmoil. He requests Chari to advise him in his disaster. 'My wife is part of me now — I did not realize it in all the years it has been happening, but I know that without her I am not whole' (198). Even after the departure of the Swamy from the town, Dandekar realizes that it is the Swamy who wins Sarojini's mind. When the dwarf returns all the materials offered by Sarojini to the Swamy, Dandekar is convinced that the real priced possessions are not the material things but Sarojini's well being. It is spiritual awakening in Dandekar that re-establishes their conjugal happiness. As Edwin Thumboo observes, "That larger bond between husband and wife that would make the relationship something more than the merely domestic has collapsed. But within this realization lies his need to have her restored to him in the fullest sense...." (183). The story ends with a sense of satisfaction in Dandekar who hastens to his children to give the good news of the recovery of their family bond and peace with the return of their beloved mother to their fold.

In *Some Inner Fury*, after Kitsamy returns from London, his family gets busy in selecting a bride for him. Premala, an embodiment of traditional Indian woman, has been approved by the entire family. Her gentle and modest ways win friends wherever he goes. Because of her loving and tender nature she tries her best to please her husband. Modelled in the pattern of the traditional Indian housewife she is not satisfied with the Westernized way of life that Kit wants her to follow. But under the pressure of her husband she is bound to wear shorts, play tennis and attend midnight parties. She is also expected to be submissive, sacrificing and obedient. Kit has extramarital relationship with an English lady but he suspects that his wife has an illicit affair with his step-brother Govind. Premala endeavours to mould herself to suit to Kit's modern tastes but Kit never tries to understand her sentiments. In her increasing alienation from his world, she associates herself with the missionary work of setting up of a school for children in a village. In order to hide her feelings of loneliness and frustration she actively participates in social welfare activities and adopts a small abandoned girl child. Kit observes, 'And from each visit she came back glowing, revived, as if her parched spirit had at last found a spring at which to refresh itself' (154). Their marriage, performed in all pomp and glamour, cannot last long due to incompatibility of their attitudes. Like Rukmani she is forced to accept all that life gives her. Govind blames Kit for her tragic predicament, "She loved you, he said, you never loved her, you don't even know the meaning of love. You gave her nothing-not even a home. You drove her to the village — you drove her to her death" (240).

Intimate human bonds are jeopardized in the absence of good understanding, free communication and mutual adjustment. Like Maya and Goutam in Anita Desai's *Cry The Peacock*. Kit and Premala fail in enjoying happy marital bliss because of their communication gap. Like Dandekar, Kit fails to grasp the value of love and faith, hence invites tragic separation. But in contrast to Premala and Sarojini, Sarala Devi in Ruth Prawar Jhabvala's novel *Get Ready For Battle* is portrayed as a rebel symbolizing woman's struggle against injustice. Jhabvala justifies Sarala's action when she escapes to her father, being utterly exasperated by a faithless, arrogant and indifferent husband.

In *The Nowhere Man* Vasantha has been characterized as a typical Hindu wife with traditional attitudes to life. When Srinivasa decides to immigrate to England he takes with him his newly married wife. Like a traditional Hindu wife Vasantha accompanies her husband with hopes of a brilliant future. She does not like to lead a gypsy life, frequently changing the dwelling places. She insists on Srinivas to buy a house and settle down, 'We, my family, have for generations been accustomed to living in a house' (17). Srinivas perceives, in her mode of living, use of custom, use of food and religious practices, a purely traditional Indian. To satisfy her desire, he buys a house in South London. Vasantha's visionary look is extended back to the old Indian joint family set up. She desires to stay together with her family members even after the marriage of the sons. She plans, 'Then the loving mother-in-law would allocate one upper floor to each son and wife, and the ground floor reserved for themselves, ageing parents who would be past climbing the stairs' (19). But unfortunately her whole plan ends in smoke. Her younger son Seshu dies in an air crash and the elder one chooses to live separately with his English wife. She gets invitation from Laxman to visit her grand son but ill-fated as she is, she cannot see the grand child as she is contaminated by tuberculosis. The mother's wounded soul can no more sustain a life of separation from the near and dear ones. In utter dejection she gets nostalgic about her native place. After severe physical suffering and mental turmoil Vasantha finally dies of consumption. In spite of all her bruises her last words are 'It has been a happy marriage' (38). As per her last desire, Srinivas performs her funeral rituals by sprinkling earth and Ganges water fondly collected from India. Thus, though she dies in a foreign land Vasantha's soul is believed to get peace when the Ganges water and the Thames water combinedly carry and wash away her final remnants. After her death Srinivas' life becomes a void. He finds himself, 'a nowhere man looking for a nowhere city' (166).

In *Two Virgins*, Amma and her widowed sister Aunt Alamelu represent the traditional Indian womanhood. As elderly women they stand opposite to the young generation of girls. They cannot accept the Christian lessons taught and dance programmes presented by the young girls in the Mission High School. As Margaret P.Joseph aptly comments :

> Aunt Alamelu is the rock of tradition, the norm of moral behaviour, and perhaps the only convincing character in the book. She is a familiar figure in the Indian joint family, combining in herself the poor relation, the widow and the interfering sister-in-law (147).

She tries to bring up Saroja, who studies in the State School, in the traditional mould of austere conduct. Both Amma and Aunt Alamelu are shocked to know that Miss Mendoza inspires Lalitha to aspire for a career of a teacher or a nurse as these professions are considered highly respectable for women in England. Their suspicion about the conduct of Mr.Gupta proves to be true as Lalitha becomes a victim to his lust. When Lalitha proposes to be an actress, Aunt Alamelu vehemently opposes the idea and cries, "You, a respectable girl, a girl from respected family..... You want to be a notch girl, a devadasi, such as no one in our line not for twenty generations has ever descended to being, is that your ambition?" (82). When Lalitha argues in a self-defensive way Aunt Alamelu gets more irritated and fumes at the child. 'I know what is going on these days, these days young people think they know best they have no respect for their elders, they have no respect for anything except their own willful ways' (82). Aunt Alamelu in utter disgust leaves the house and goes to some holy place to spend her last days in peace.

Saroja is portrayed as a contrast to Lalitha, like the two sisters Elizabeth and Lydia in Jane Austen's *Pride and Prejudice* and Elinor and Mariannna in *Sense and Sensibility*. Saroja resists all temptations that ruin her sister. She learns about sex by observing Amma and Manikkam's wife. She is well aware of her feminine body growing into maturity. She is much influenced by Aunt Alamelu's moral instructions and her old traditional values. She never argues strongly with the superiors. She is never swayed away by emotionalism or by vague aspirations. Rather she feels pity for her sister who has been victimized by the malevolent corrupting forces of the city. She resists the sexual advances made by Chingleput and Devraj and reacts strongly 'What do you take me for, she screamed, a virgin in your whore-house?' (245). The story ends with Saroja maturing into a wise and responsible girl, 'She is no more afraid. She knew too much, she had gone through too much to be afraid of anything' (250). Now that she is grown up, she is conscious of her own safety and self-respect. She is in fact a happy compromise between the older generation and the younger one. Shanta Krishnaswamy comments on her,

'Saroja symbolizes the conflict between reason and feeling, between tradition and modernity' (219).

Rukmani, Nalini, Premala and Saroja represent the concepts of ideal Indian womanhood in terms of their willing submission to the traditional roles in the family. While Rukmani and Nalini are destined to negotiate with poverty and deprivation, Premala and Saroja are lured into living a life they totally dislike. While the women of the working class, despite privation, cling stubbornly to the traditional values of chastity and sacrifice, the middle class women, Premala and Saroja, resist resolutely the tendency to overstep the limits of their social class by refusing to compromise with social decorum and moral principles.

II

Two Virgins is a poignant tale of two girls growing up in the changing ethos of Indian life that tends to subvert traditional attitudes and is assertive of the freedom of women. As Alice Drum states :

> In *Two Virgins*, Kamala Markandaya uses the exigencies of life in the rapidly changing world of a modern Indian village to give fresh treatment to a common human problem and a familiar literary theme, coming of age (323).

In free India women enjoy political right, right to education and to job. Higher education brings noticeable change in attitudes and beliefs. The old order of suppression of women has yielded place to the new careers open for them. There is a significant shift from an attitude that "has denied woman the possibility of being a '*She*' a person capable of achieving individuation" (Ramamoorthi, 115) to an attitude that seeks to assert a distinct feminine identity.

Indian women have been traditionally portrayed as the paragon of resignation and patient suffering. Binodini, in Tagore's *Chokerbali* (1903) translated into English as *Binodini* is perhaps the first Indian woman who rebels against the social norms, claiming an identity of her own at a time when widows are socially ostracized. Binodini is an unconventional, bold character who loves Mahendra, a married man, though ultimately she submits herself to the social code of self-denial and self-sacrifice. In contrast to her, in *Ghare Baire* (1916) translated as *The Home and The World* Tagore shows in Bimala a traditional housewife who cannot extend her love beyond the strict Hindu social system.

Lalitha, in *Two Virgins*, assumes a superior air in relation to her younger sister Saroja who is mild, obedient, timid and tradition-bound. Appa is proud of his beautiful girl Lalitha who is given education in Mission High School under the guidance of Miss Mendoza. Her talent as an artist has been recognised by her teacher. She advises Saroja enthusiastically, 'you have to seize your opportunity before it passes you by, you have to be quick in your answers, if you want to get anywhere' (77). But Saroja is not so daring and dashing to easily accept her sister's advice. When Lalitha tries to persuade her parents to allow her to join films, they hesitate as they are not quite sure about her new venture. As an ambitious young girl, Lalitha is strongly inspired by Mr. Gupta, the film director. To the vehement objections of Aunt Alamelu, she retorts, '...These days girls from respectable families act in film, can I help it if an old fossil like you haven't heard?' (82). Finally, Lalitha, the pet of Appa, is successful in seizing the opportunity to become a film star. Looking down upon the rural living, she escapes into the glamorous urban life. But soon she is victimized for her lack of experience and wisdom. Instead of getting recognition she turns into a problem for the parents when there is the need to rescue her from unwanted pregnancy. In utter disgrace she tries to disappear in the huge crowd of the city as she does not like to lead a dull and dreary life in the undeveloped rural setting. In R.K. Narayan's *The Guide* Rosie is successful as a dancer, achieves her goal as a careerist whereas Lalitha's identity as a dancer is lost in an illusory world. Anita Desai's protagonist, Sita in *Where Shall We Go This Summer*? realizes in her middle age the futility of her rebellion against her trapped and subjugated living. Rashmi in Nayantara Sahgal's *This Time of Morning* (1968) is individualist, strong-willed, sensitive and intelligent. Her liberated self getting separated from Dillip seems to find comfort and security in another man, Rakesh. Women like Indu in Sashi Deshpande's *Root and*

Shadows (1983) and Saru in *That Long Silence* (1988) revolt against parental authority. But too much of autonomy leads them to break marital ties and to engage themselves in extra-marital affairs. Thus, the so called liberated women ultimately lose themselves in the darkness of an unfeeling world.

In *Some Inner Fury* Mira develops a trend different from Premala. She is brought up in an anglicized manner, though, she belongs to a traditional Hindu home. Kit's English friend Richard stays in their family and develops attachment towards Mira. Richard is quite gentle, reasonable and disciplined. He awaits the permission of Mira's parents for marriage. Mira's mother in her conservative way wants to postpone the event explaining that she is too young to marry. Differences of race and culture do not however stand as an impediment. But soon their romantic relationship gets disturbed by the political unrest caused by the Indian revolutionaries. During their nation-wide tour they realize that the Britishers are no more wanted in India. Mira is now faced with a dilemma. The processionists' slogan inspires her tremendously. She is confirmed that she can no more adjust with Richard. Finally, in the mob fury they are naturally separated from each other. Richard has never ill-treated her inspite of the political differences. Rather at the time of national upheaval he steadily stands by her. At the time of Kit's death he gives her moral support and consolation. It is Mira who forsakes her love on patriotic ground. In the court room when Govind is declared free she is overwhelmed with joy and a sense of victory. At this moment, she realizes, 'This was not a time for decision, for he knew he could not come with me, and I know I cannot stay; it was simply the time for departing' (285). With the dreams shattered, Mira can do nothing but console herself, 'What had been given us had been gifted freely, abundantly, lit with a splendour which had coloured and enriched our whole living, it could never be taken from us' (285). Thus, the strong and harmonious emotional bond of Mira and Richard is breached under political and national compulsions. Like Lalitha, Mira emerges from her adolescence into the full womanliness of passionate love and reaches the climatic point where she is pathetically withdrawn from love. Haydn Moore Willilams comments on her, 'The impulse to freedom in her character is foretold in her leaving home to become a journalist under the wing of an emancipated woman who is also a dedicated nationalist' (169).

Lady Caroline Bell is the most dominating figure in *Possession.* The rich, beautiful, aristocratic, fashionable divorced lady is strangely attracted towards a poor, rustic, uneducated goatherd boy. Caroline is extremely charmed by Val's artistic talent. As soon as she recognizes his talent she decides to take him to London. The most willful and obstinate lady Caroline pays heavily to his parents as a compensation of their loss of a son. In London, Caroline is possessed by the sensual desire for Val. Finally, she is successful in moulding the boy into a talented artist. He learns to speak good English and manages with guests invited to parties. Caroline is fully satisfied as she possesses Val physically and intellectually. Initially Val is excited at the new prospects open to him but soon he loses all enthusiasm for life and art. He realizes that his artistic life thrives under Caroline's protection and patronage. A boy from a poor background feels alien in Caroline's prosperous society. Amidst all material comforts he feels spiritually defunct. He discovers her selfish obsession for possession. Her vision cannot go beyond gold and money. Most inhumanly she exerts her devilish power in adopting tricks, forgery and sex relations. Caroline's diabolic intents drive her to the extent of snatching his true love for Annabel and killing Ellie who bears his child. Finally, when he realizes that Caroline does not care for him but his artistic output which fetches money, prestige and power he feels anguished, repentant and leaves the seductive woman for good. He returns to his childhood mentor, the Swamy under whose spiritual guidance he regains his mental health. As P.S. Chauhan Comments :

> That despite her glamour, her wealth and her seductions, Valmiki has left her for the bleak cave of the Swamy, speaks of the defeat of all that Caroline and her society had represented, clever talk, sensuous living, material comforts and career opportunities (140).

In *The Coffer Dams*, the focus of the narrative is on Helen who is caught between two different systems of values, beliefs and attitudes. In the rural and tribal setting of the fast changing post-colonial India, the narrative highlights the confrontation between the East and the West. Clinton and Helen springing from the same cultural background and placed in a comfortable state of living are estranged because Helen unlike Rukmani and Nalini is confronted with the choice between her own will and surrender to her husband's will and whims. As Clinton is obsessed with his construction works to achieve personal glory at the cost of the innocent hard working tribal people, his wife Helen is all compassion and love for the poor tribal folk.

Clinton, the British Engineer, in charge of building the coffer dam considers himself as only a builder, a technocrat but his wife is a young, vivacious and spirited woman who looks around for a few moments of relief in the tribal wilderness. In the early part of the novel the couple are found happy and contented. Clinton expects from her an identification with his grand responsibility where as she identifies herself with the tribal life. Gradually they drift apart from each other. Clinton regards the tribal workers insignificant and barbarous. Helen, on the other hand, gets more and more involved in the day to day life of the natives. She says. "I just think of them as human beings" and suggests to Clinton, "You've got to get beyond their skins" (12). Thus, Clinton and Helen stand diametrically opposed in their attitudes towards men and life. Helen is naturally attracted towards Bashiam, the tribal technocrat who is a meeting point of modernity and the archetypal world of tribals. A strange bond of friendship and love develops between them. As R.K. Srivastava remarks, "It is a symbolic union of the East and the West, of primitivism and civilization" (11). Coming in close contact with Bashiam, Helen is immensely transformed. She is dissociated from the dehumanized world of Clinton. She experiences a sense of fulfillment, getting liberated from the clutches of male chauvinism.

Like Dr. Kenny, Helen devotes herself to the welfare of the undeveloped, uneducated, poor tribal workers in India. She extends her heart and hand to solve their problems. She fights against their exploitation. She is charmed by their life of instincts and emotions which she misses in the so-called civilized society. Gradually she is totally drawn towards the tribes, respecting their beliefs and customs. She argues with Clinton for the recovery of the bodies of the two workers who die in an accident but Clinton takes it lightly. When the issue takes a serious turn and the entire work stops, he realizes his wife's foresightedness and the workers' sensitiveness. Helen admonishes the arrogant husband, "Can't you care? Don't human beings matter anything to you?" (105). She accuses him of being inhuman. But Clinton remains silent and indifferent. He thinks that the natives are animals and they are used to suffering and death. To him their death is an accident, a small incident. Helen with her kindred spirit seeks harmony in an alien culture. The novel ends with a note of realization and reconciliation. After Bashiam's accident, the project work being complete, Helen comes back to her husband forgetting all her earlier experience of disintegration and dissatisfaction.

Mrs. Pickering in *The Nowhere Man* exhibits the finer elements of western civilization. She appears in the life of Srinivas when he is on the verge of committing suicide to escape the anguish of utter loneliness. With her charming personality and persuasive words she conquers the heart of the hopeless man and wins his confidence. She encourages him to seek sustenance from the land of his adoption, 'If one is cut off from one's culture, there is always the adopted one to draw upon' (68). Mrs. Pickering can achieve what Vasantha could not do with her superstitious views and religious sentiments. Srinivas realizes that there is possibility of one's adaptability to a foreign land. Though an English lady, she can compensate his loss of wife, sons and the native country. Srinivas becomes aware of belonging to a great human society. Mrs. Pickering lives with him, inspite of public criticism, as a caretaker of his household, a sympathizer, a counsellor and a kind-hearted benefactor. She steadily stands by him when her countrymen agitate against him. It is her hospitality and tender nursing that sustain his life. But all her good will and safety measures are over-powered by the stronger antagonistic forces of the diabolic agents causing his death. Ironically the evil-doer, the racist Fred has himself been victimized. All his racial hatred ends in smoke. When Mrs. Glass, Srinivas' neighbour is horrified at the untoward, unexpected incident, Mrs. Pickering explains, 'Blame myself.... Why should I? I cared for him' (299). She glorifies the British practice of liberalism and humanism. Uma Parameswaran aptly comments :

> Personal relationships are Kamala Markandaya's forte. Step by step she builds up relationships, analyses them and dramatically makes them represent something larger than themselves. In *The Nowhere Man* the relationship between Mrs. Pickering and Srinivas could be read as the relationship between the best of India and the best of Britain (124).

Along with Dr. Radcliffe and constable Kent, Mrs. Pickering stands as representative of the West who can withstand racial prejudices, personal afflictions and help the destitute.

In *The Golden Honeycomb* Kamala Markandaya has created some memorable women characters who play significant roles in the freedom struggle. They decide the destiny of the Princely State with their wide social and cultural awakening. The Dowager Queen Manjula and commoner queen Mohini with their sharp wit, pragmatic sense and reasonableness can change the traditional system in the political history of the state. They can inspire the younger generation with national fervour. After the accidental death of Bawajiraj II, the young Prince Bawajiraj III ascends the throne of Devapur state. The Mother Queen Manjula practically acts as the power behind the throne. The British Agent and the Dewan cannot exercise their free hand in public or private issues without her knowledge. The Queen Mother observes that the princes are deliberately trained in the pattern of English gentlemen to keep them loyal. She has all sympathy for the poor. She is interested in solving common men's problems. She does not appreciate her son to be educated in the Western manner. She sets the first royal rebellion by insisting on suckling her own baby by herself, contrary to the royal tradition. In spite of her husband's persuasions, she defies royal conventions. She is unhappy when her son is inclined towards the alien government, ignorant of and insensitive to the problems of the people of the land. However, she is satisfied in selecting a bride for her son according to her choice. As the pretty wife Shanta Devi cannot contribute a son for the continuation of the dynasty, the king

Bawajiraj III is granted special assent to marry a girl from the common level of society.

Mohini, the commoner beloved of the king is persuaded by the Queen Mother not to assume the status of a queen. She prefers to be his concubine, a status that guarantees her freedom to bring up her son. The exchange of their views has been dramatically presented :

"You could be a queen."
'I don't want to be your queen, I want to be free.'
'Am I not free?'
'Of course, you're not free,'
'As far as I'm aware —'

'You're aware of nothing. The British have tied you up hand and foot and you don't even know it. Do you want me to be shackled like you?' (32).

Thus securing a free status, Mohini enjoys the privilege to influence the King. Her position is further strengthened when the King is blessed with a son. Mohini's son Rabindranath is now accepted as the heir-apparent. Bawajiraj III feels confused at the attitudes of his mother and Mohini towards the state and the Emperor. Though he sticks to his principles and traditional forms of royalty, he has no option but to yield to the demands of Manjula and Mohini in the matter of education of Rabi by an Indian Pandit rather then by an Englishman. Rabi's identification with India's indigenous culture is cultivated through a deliberate and careful nursing by his mother and grand-mother.

Rabi grows as a contrast to his father. His friendship with Janaki, the sweeper girl, his stay in Jaya's hut during the mill-workers' strike give him specific knowledge of women and of common man's problems. When he returns to Devapur, his vision is clear and his determination to improve the lot of the impoverished multitude is stronger. In due course of time, the King and the Agent become aware of the emergence of a generation of youth led by Manjula, Mohini, the Dewan and the Pandit. The youthful Rabi, Usha, Das and Janaki organize peaceful demonstrations against the alien Government. When Mohini requests Rabi to be gentle towards his father who tries to crush the agitation by exercising his administrative power, Rabi answers sarcastically, 'Be gentle. The Maharaja in purple and the British in scarlet. Wealth accumulating while men decayed, Be gentle' (423). Finally, Rabi along with Usha undertakes a mission to stand by the suffering people. Mohini is pleased to see her ambition fulfilled. Manjula and Mohini succeed in bringing up Rabi in the traditional spirit of humanism and freedom. As A.V. Krishna Rao rightly observes :

> Manjula and Mohini play roles in the affirmation of the continuity of the essential cultural values amid the myriad political changes in modern India. They represent the best of India's traditional womanhood in guiding and shaping the destiny of Bawaji Raj III and Rabindranath, who, in their turn provide peace and progress to the people of their state (The novels, 238).

Rabi is inspired by Sophie, the beautiful daughter of the Copelands and Usha, the Dewan's youngest daughter. Together they lead the agitation against alien rule and tyranny. In collaboration with the two girls Rabi engages himself with many acts of public service. But like Mira's tragic separation from Richard, Sophie's love is also withdrawn for racial reasons. Rabi is also convinced of her lack of sentiments and warm feeling for the Indians. He realizes that his life's partner can be no other than Usha, "A woman of a pared and lucid grace with whom he could talk, or be still, who could move him, and move with him, effortlessly picking up where he left off, their common strand" (455).

Lalitha, Mira, Majula and Mohini represent the new generation of Indian women who assert their distinct feminine identity in the face of a hostile society which resists all attempts to grant moral and social freedom to women. These characters in Kamala Markandaya's fiction, who belong to an affluent section of society, embody the post-colonial aspirations of Indian women to realize selfhood through uninhibited freedom. Caroline, Helen and Mrs. Pickering are another interesting group of women characters who are aliens in India but who demonstrate a rare sense of compassion and love for the poor and oppressed Indians. They represent the contradictions within colonial power in terms of attitudes towards India. While the hardcore colonialists tend to exploit, tyrannize and subvert, these English women have a strong faith in human values and abiding human relationships.

III

Women, in Kamala Markandaya's novels, fall into a distinct two fold pattern : those who belong to the economically poor and middle class society and those who belong to an affluent and upper class society. While the former group behaves in traditional ways of quiet and helpless acceptance of pain and suffering, the latter group stands up against injustice to women and asserts a distinct identity for the Indian women in terms of close participation in social and political events and movements.

3

Crisis of Transition

Post-colonial Indian fiction in English embodies various images of the Indian society in terms of its traditional values and practices as well as its changing ethos in the process of its transition from an agrarian to an industrialized and urbanized socio-economic order. While novelists like Anita Desai and Ruth Prawar Jhabvala are basically concerned with the problems of urbanization, Kamala Markandaya is chiefly preoccupied with the problems of tragic encounter between the traditional Indian values and cultural practices on the one hand, and the industrial and urban outlook on the other. This chapter is an attempt at exploring Kamala Markandaya's critique of

(a) the village,
(b) the family and
(c) the socio-cultural tensions in the context of an intercultural encounter.

II

The hierarchy of social classes in Indian villages is based on distinctions of caste and financial status in the context of an agrarian society. As B. Kuppuswamy aptly summarizes :

> Since, the village economy is based primarily on agriculture, the ownership of land gives rise to an agrarian class structure. There are the land-owners who form the upper-class on account of their wealth and proprietorship. There is the middle-class consisting of the tenants who take the land on lease for cultivation from the landlords, and there are the

> agricultural labourers who are employed on a daily wage basis by the landlords or the tenants to help them in the cultivation of the land (475-76).

Thus, landowners, farmers and traders constitute the core of the traditional Indian rural community. War and change of regime have, of course, affected the village communities in the system of land tenure, land holding and occupations. But what has essentially happened is that the village life is in the process of far-reaching socio-economic changes in its encounter with urban sub-culture. The landlord in the erstwhile Zemindari system was a rich person who was wealthy at the cost of the poor farmers and workers who were deprived of the basic needs of living. The archetype of the landlord suggests exploitation of the poor by a wealthy villager who enjoys social power. The money-lenders held an important place in the rural economy. In times of natural calamity such as famine, draught and flood, the poor farmers and workers were forced to borrow money from professional money-lenders at a very high rate of interest. Sometimes the villagers pawned their land and house to these money lenders and more often than not, they never got them back, for they could never pay back the loan.

In post-colonial India, industrialists, factory owners and businessmen are replacing the landlords and money-lenders. Industrialization is seen as the only viable source of wealth for the individual and the country. Mills and factories provide better job opportunity to young people. Transport and communication facilities have led to greater mobility and interaction with cities and the urban folk. It is this transition from the agrarian to an industrial and urban society which engages Kamala Markandaya in most of her fiction.

Kamala Markandaya's fiction often reflects deep sense of loss and a sad brooding over destruction of the calm and idyllic beauty of the countryside caused by the din and bustle of urbanization. *Nectar in a Sieve* embodies this tone of loss. It is nostalgic depiction of the traditional rural ethos in the perspective of a radical social transition. The blue skies, green plants and running brook have been a perennial source of delight for the villagers.

But now birds, sparrows, bulbuls, parrots are hardly seen. The cool silence and tranquility is disturbed by the clamour of bullock carts with loads of brick, stone and cement. There are references to the milking of cows and goats, churning of butter and milk, planting beans, potatoes, brinjals and chilies. Rukmani is engaged in pounding red chilies into powder, collecting dung for fuel and making dung cakes. The villagers have simple food habits. Their meal consists of plain boiled rice, dal, vegetables and curds. In their good harvest days, Rukmani remembers, 'There was food in plenty for two people and we ate well : rice for morning and evening means, dal, sometimes a coconut grated fine and cooked in milk and sugar; some times a wheat cake, fried in butter and melting in the mouth' (13). On special occasions such as celebrations of births and marriages villagers spend lavishly beyond their means. Rukmani's sisters and her daughter after their marriage leave the parents penniless.

In *Two Virgins* Kamala Markandaya presents a graphic picture of the beautiful nature scenes in the villages. The plantation on the roadside of the village serves multiple purpose. The travellers take rest in the shade of the Banyan trees. Saroja along with the boys enjoys swinging in the branches of the trees. Amma is fond of the Tamarind as it yields 'enormous quantities of tamarind for her pickles and for sale' (16). Saroja likes its sweet and sour taste. Chingleput collects tamarind for his recipes. The biggest threat to the rural vegetation comes from the monkeys. They come when the tress are loaded with fruits, the papayas ripening, the gourds fattening on Manikkam's wife's vegetable patch. The villagers struggle hard to save their fruits from the monkeys, in hot days when mangoes ripe. Amma prepares pickle.

In contrast to the peasants' thatched huts and mud walls, the tannery building is made of brick and cement. Markandaya draws the reader's attention to the villagers' fortitude, courage, uncomplaining acceptance of good and evil alike, their extreme attachment to the land and devotion to their profession. Nathan and Rukmani suffer calamity together. They experience agony in the city where they receive help from a stranger boy Puli in their starvation but not from their own sons. Coming out of her father's mansion, Rukmani faces difficulties in her husband's mud hut, but soon she adjusts herself to the situation and assures him, 'It suits me quite well to live here' (10). Initially, Rukmani seems contented with her married life with Nathan's granary full of paddy :

> While the sun shines on you and the field are green and beautiful to the eye, and your husband sees beauty in you which no one has seen before, and you have a good store of grain laid away for hard times, a roof over you and a sweet stirring in your body, what more can a woman ask for? (12).

But she feels emotionally disturbed when a revolutionary change comes over the village by the establishment of the tannery. She reflects :

> Change I had known before, and it has been gradual....
> But the change that now came into my life, into all our lives, blasting its way into our village, seemed wrought in the twinkling of an eye (29).

However, people accept this radical change. When the factory affects agriculture and the cottage industries, people tend to migrate to the towns in search of employment. Chingleput, the sweet maker, the weavers, the blacksmith apprehend sharp decline in sales of hand-made things. But the blacksmith in *Two Virgins* is still unrelenting, 'No machine, he said, could be fashioned to do what he did, he was not afraid of machines usurping him which was the great fear of the weavers in the village' (79).

The young and subtle mind of Saroja is so much disturbed by the change that she secretly but sincerely prays God 'not to allow machines into their village which would destroy Chingleput and his skills' (80). Saroja in her visit to the city gets so much upset and bewildered that she wants to run away to her village and never come back to the city. She is assured :

> At home there were fields to rest your eyes on, colours that changed with the seasons. The tender green of new crops, the tawny shades of harvest, the tints of freshly turned earth, you could have told the week and the month of the year by these alone (243).

She is so well acquainted with the well, the fields, the grove, the water meadow and the inhabitants of the village that she never apprehends to be lost, whereas, in the city she gets irritated at the suspicious looks of the strangers and realizes why and how her sister Lalitha gets herself lost there. She feels quite at home and notices every thing usual and normal when she comes back to her village. There is a note of contentment when she looks at the grain store filled with sacks of paddy, the courtyard properly maintained with sprinkled water and the dust being swept, the buffalo shed and the field itself.

When young men of the villages realize that the land is no more reliable in providing them sustenance, gradually they leave behind their hereditary professions and migrate to towns. Rama Jha observes, 'Victims of the cash Nexus, they don't adjust well with the change around them. Rukmani's whole family is affected by this change. Nathan is in a helpless plight, whereas his sons are leaving for the city' (164). The tannery is not to be blamed alone for the change. The peasants for their traditional intimacy and sentimental attachment as well as their dependence on land, have an instinctive sense of nature's cycles of creation and preservation. As Rukmani explains :

> And whatever extraneous influence the tannery may have exercised, the calamities of the land belong to it alone, born of wind and rain and weather, immensities not to be tempered by man or his creations (136).

Nature has been presented both in its beauty and harshness. Nathan's coconut plant is destroyed in stormy weather. People are killed by lightning as they seek shelter under a tree. Kali's hut is completely destroyed with the roof blown away and the mud walls crumbled. The rain becomes the symbol of 'disaster and desolation' (45) : trees uprooted, paddy crushed, sticks and stones scattered, huts demolished, shops destroyed and cats, dogs and bats dead. Rukmani is aware of the stark reality, 'To those who live by the land there must always come times of hardship, of fear and of hunger, even as there are years of plenty' (136).

In the backdrop of this rural landscape, there is excitement and jubilation at the prospects of a better living. Kunthi asks Rukmani, 'Are you not glad that our village is no longer a clump of huts but a small town?' (33). She hopes that the shops, tea stalls and bioscope would soon be available in their locality.

Kunthi, Kali and Janaki feel the importance of the tannery as they confess that the land can no more sustain all their sons. Gradually, the tannery stands as a great landmark of progress. In *Two virgins* Appa and his sons heartily welcome machines. Chingleput is convinced of the benefit of machine. He finds the town full of machines and the machines work better as 'They spun sugar finer, faster, than he with his prongs. They roasted nuts by the barrelful' (4). Amidst such mixed reactions the traditional village advances towards inevitable urbanization. R.M. Varma rightly comments :

> With the process of industrialization, there are conflicts, heart burning and troubles, no doubt, but the society changes, and change it will. Every society will industrialize. Inspite of the great resistance offered to it by inherited structures and others, which may help to keep some of the traditional, cultural aspects of life, still living (31).

In *The Coffer Dams* a small industrial town has been built up on the 'uniform, impenetrable green' (8) of the hillside. In order to construct a dam on the turbulent river, the jungles and hills need to be destroyed. The face of the village is completely changed with rapid construction of the 'workshop and work buildings, loading and unload bays, the car maintenance sheds, the workers' quarters, the engineers' bungalows, the amenity buildings, the water tower, ice and filtration plant, pumping and power stations' (9). But in spite of the ravage of nature by machinery, the inhabitants co-operate with the technocrats as both excess rain and scarcity of rain on the land cause havoc. The river cannot help the villagers in the time of draught. In the floods, their mud huts are dissolved and washed away. After the dam is set up, the river banks stand firm in the face of heavy monsoon rains. Hence, Gopal Rao, the Indian assistant admits, 'The dams were built for the benefit of the people' (217). Ramesh Chandha rightly points out Markandaya's skilful way of presenting 'a pulsating record of human suffering and cultural consciousness against the backdrop of formidable elements of Nature' (63).

For Rukmani, tannery is a sinister presence, even though she is aware that the real causes of ruin of her family are inclement weather, famine, crop failure, landlordism, money lending system and defective land tenure system. Rukmani is literate and intelligent enough to realize the problems of the villagers brought about by industrialization and urbanization that devastates village economy and communal living. Janaki's husband cannot compete with the city shopkeepers. Chingleput, is shocked at the sharp decline of his business. Amidst utter disaster and failure, Ravi finally realizes that one is bound to remain backward unless one copes with emerging outlook of gross materialism that has already gripped the rural setting. In *The Coffer Dams* in spite of the loss of human lives and sensibility the machines prevail over man for sheer materialistic gains.

Kamala Markandaya's perception of the Indian village is in terms of a nostalgia for the rural outlook that valued human and humane considerations as basic to a healthy community. Her observations of the Indian village are informed by an awareness of an emerging social order governed by machines, factories, trade and business.

III

Social scientist S.C. Dube while analyzing the Indian family system points out that 'Togetherness and solidarity within the family are much lauded virtues' (67). In the past when people lived entirely on agriculture, joint families were quite stable with each member participating in the process of earning livelihood. But with the rapid growth of population, agriculture is not more capable of sustaining the family. This causes not only growing poverty in Indian villages but a tendency to migrate to cities in search of prosperity. Ravi's father, a tenant farmer cannot provide sustenance to his children. His mother sorrowfully observes, 'One after another they had been forced out, and had gone, three sons, her daughter, her son-in-law, all in turn had boarded the train that bore them away to the city' (26). Similar circumstances compel Arjun and Thambi to explain to their parents about their decision to go to Ceylon Tea plantation. Arjun argues with his mother. 'There is nothing for us here, for we have neither the means to buy land not to rent it, would you have us wasting our youth, chafing against things we cannot change?' (72). The village youth are impelled to escape the melieu where the rich and selfish Zamindars thrive, ruthless agents like Sivaji, cunning merchants like Hanuman and money-lenders like Biswas and Perumal prosper. The old parents like Nathan and Rukmani are left behind with their 'hot and bitter' tears, 'springs of sorrow' and 'tortured feelings' (72). In *Two Virgins* Appa allows his sons and even his daughter Lalitha to go to the city in search of a more meaningful existence. In *Possession* the Swamy grants permission to Val to leave his village and family with the hope that Val's talent would find scope and opportunity to grow and flourish. In the advanced environment of the Western civilization, the unlearned goatherd boy from an unknown South Indian village is able to acquire all modern sophistication and achieve recognition of his artistic talent. In *The Nowhere Man* Srinivas' ancestral house known as the 'Chandraprasad' refers not only to the building, but also to integrated, indivisible family ties. The solid structure is built under the supervision of Srinivas' grand father, who was 'a Brahmin land owner, descendant of a long line of learned men' (99). He sold his village house and moved to the town with his wife, two sons and two daughters with a view to giving better education to the children. Srinivas has a kind of emotional attachment for the house. Later the family gets separated from the house as Srinivas is forced to leave India under political constraints. But taking refuge in England the family gets further disintegrated because of the racial and cultural clashes. Vasantha's ambitious plans to house the entire family under one roof ironically falls flat when every one of the family gradually falls apart from each other. Thus there is eventually a total breakdown of the joint family.

Dr. Kenny, the voice of modernity, tries to make the peasants aware of the limitations of their conventional beliefs and prejudices. He explains to them the value of family planning and the dangers implied in their faith that having a large family is a matter of honour and pride. Janaki, the wife of the village shop-keeper has seven children. Rukmani feels proud in giving birth to one daughter and six sons. But subsequently under heavy economic pressures the large family disintegrates as the children move out to cities and adopt urban ways of life. Ravi gets himself separated from his in-laws when he feels suffocated with so many people living on his single income. Contrary to family traditions, young men like Laxman and Murugan choose their own brides without parental consent. Murugan violates the orthodox sexual and family code by whimsically abandoning his wife and children. Nathan treats his daughter Ira harshly and contemptuously when she resorts to prostitution. Like Ira, Ammu, Murugan's deserted wife, justifies her immoral conduct as a successful way of living, 'One must live, she repeated, defiant, challenging, sensing reproach where none could be; for it is very true, one must live'(164). Sacrabani, Ira's albino child is the symbol of this attitude : a willing marriage between necessity and free will. Trying to surmount the pain and hunger of poverty, Ira and Ammu drown their conscience in the welter of utilitarian society. Kamala Das in her story collection *A Doll of the Child Prostitute* (1977) presents similar predicament of young, innocent girls. Radha, Sita, Mira, Saraswati and Laxshmi are all victims of poverty who submit themselves to flesh trade with the hope of a materially comfortable living. Sita meets premature death. Poverty compels Sindhathai to perform abortion for as little as twenty rupees in order to make living. Lalitha is also forced to abort her foetus after being duped by the city tradesmen. Ira ventures to defy traditional sense of morality like Sonia in Dostoevsky's *Crime and Punishment*. Her conscience is clear. She justifies her struggle for existence, 'Tonight and tomorrow and every night, so long there is need' (99). Selvam's sympathy, his act of providing shelter to Ira and her son is untenable in terms of the traditional norms of social conduct. Ravi gets into Damodar's crime net to overcome the anguish of poverty and Damodar is an unrepentant bootlegger devoid of any moral conscience. As Iyengar rightly observes, what creates this moral crisis is the existence of :

> The insensitiveness of the affluent, their mania for conspicuous consumption, their hardness of heart, the exploitation of small fish by big, the worker by the capitalist, the Apus of the world by the Big shops in Mount Road, and the internal success of the bootlegger, the black-marketeer, the drug-peddler at the cost of the poor, the down and out, the desperate (445-46).

Ravi represents the new generation of young men who cannot stand firmly on tradition nor can fit into the world of competitors. His big dream of living a life of luxury is strongly threatened by his moral scruples. Damodar, who enjoys all earthly pleasures by burglary, bootlegging and smuggling looks at Ravi as a total failure having 'no heart, no lights, no guts' (232). He refuses entry to a man like Ravi with moral dilemma to his underworld. R.K. Srivastava comments :

> The competitive world of business becomes identified with Damodar's world of violence, also called a jungle, wherein he had no burden of any family and children, no qualms and no traditions. But Ravi, unlike Damodar, belongs to a jungle of civilization in which he cannot even fight freely because of his sense of honour, and of the respectability of his wife and children (Symbolic, 191).

In *A Silence of Desire* the withered Tulsi plant signifies the moral decay of Dandekar who puts his carnal pleasures and personal comforts above spiritual values. A selfish and degenerate Dandekar suspects his wife ignoring her desires and well-being. In *Two Virgins* Lalitha never passes through moral dilemma even though she keeps illicit relations with Gupta. She accepts it as an essential part of fame and glamour. She has been portrayed more as a rebel against tradition and social taboos than as a violator of moral code.

Kamala Markandaya's fiction embodies a sharp critique of the Indian family in all its moral and materialistic dimensions. Her novels, in fact, revolve round the vanishing system of well — knit family ties that gradually break down by being continually crushed by the pressures of utilitarianism, consumerism and carnal pleasures. As A.V. Krishna Rao aptly comments :

> It is possible to trade out in her novels an intelligible pattern of ideas, that reveals her aesthetic assimilation of a long established tradition under the disturbing impact of modernity (Feminine, 58).

IV

The traditional Indian society has been passing through a phase of transformation with the western ideologies and systems affecting the Indian attitudes and life styles. With the process of anglicization that started in the mid nineteenth century, India is in a process of cultural transformation. There is a clearly perceptible change from dogma and orthodoxy to modernism and material prosperity. A close study of Kamala Markandaya's novels reveals the nature of this socio-cultural transformation in terms of its reflection in the changing attitudes and ways of life and living of her characters. Characters like Kit, Mira, Roshan, Val, Dandekar, Laxman, Bawajiraj III and Lalitha are too obviously anglicized Indians who identify success with westernisation. Fred Fletcher and Richard Clinton act as anti-Indian Britishers who nurture rancour and bitter racial feelings. In contrast to them there are some British sympathizers like Dr. Kenny, Dr. Radcliffe, Mrs. Pickering and Helen who are deeply concerned with the squalor and distress of Indians. There are also staunch Indian nationalists like Govind and Rabindranath who rebel against colonial and western attitudes.

Kit is a typical westernized young man. After getting educated in Oxford, when he returns home, he finds it extremely difficult to adjust himself to the Indian conditions. Having lived for a long time in London, he admires every thing British. When he complains about the hot Indian climate, his mother advises him to learn to tolerate Indian heat. She remarks, 'He will have to make a lot of adjustments' (11). Kit has imbibed a highly anglicized attitude to life. He drinks beer, brings with him the English mannerisms and Oxford gossip. He violates Indian conventions and customs in selecting a bride of his own choice. Premala stays in Kit's family before she is accepted as the bride. She is always pressurized to adopt modern and western postures and manners. While Richard, the British, prefers to wear Indian clothes, Kit chooses suit and tie. Indian ceremonies fatigue him. The décor of his house is entirely European. As Mira observes :

> Kit's house was different, the furnishing had been left in the hands of a European firm, and there was nothing that was Indian about it. There were wilton carpets on the floor, wing chairs and a cocktail cabinet in the drawing room Chintzes in the bed rooms, the side-board held English bone china and of

> the Pahari Miniatures, Premala had collected and the Kasha rugs, she had been given there was no sign (97).

In India, Kit is appointed as a Collector, a senior member of the civil service, a part of the highest bureaucracy of the government. He loves the life of parties and clubs. Even though he defends Hinduism against Christian missionary activities, he does not think it worth while to participate in Hindu rituals. He does not appreciate Govind's revolutionary activities aimed at ousting the British from India. Like Krishna in Bal Chandra Rajan's *The Dark Dancer,* Kit feels himself alienated in his native land. As a Cambridge product he finds himself a total stranger in his own country. This maladjustment leads both Kit and his Indian wife Premala to their tragic end. O.P. Saxena remarks, 'Kit is typical alienated person who is only a vine clinging to the British Raj, having no individual identity of his own' (78). Kit's father, who is a member of the British club, enjoys some rare amenities, keeping himself loyal to the British interest in India. Persons like him have big mansions with gardens and lawns and a host of servants. They spend Indian summers in hilly resorts. In the company of the Britishers they play golf, bridge and billiards and drink at the bar. Their life of revelries resembles the upper middle-class life in Jane Austin's *Emma* with Randall's party, Box Hill Party, ball dances in Crown inn, eating, dancing, chatting and merry-making. In the modern Indian society the upper class continues to enjoy the privileges that people like Kit's father obtain as loyal servants of the rich and the powerful.

In *Possession* Val is elevated from his goatherd existence to the sophisticated London life. But when he realizes that he is exploited for the selfish gains of Caroline, he frees himself from her mundane spell and comes back to the Swamy. However, Western influenced he may be his artistic self is essentially rooted in India. Harish Raizada aptly observes :

> Notwithstanding the powerful influence of the west on him, Val is never able to alienate himself completely from his Indian roots. It is evident from the divine urge which finds expression even through the paintings drawn by him under the secular influence of the West (57).

Jumbo is presented as an ex-prince of a small state in India. He visits England and enjoys his time there in luxurious living. He has been thoroughly metamorphosed into a western man. He is intimate with the British and organizes cocktail parties. After independence, with the dissolution of princely states, Jumbo, like his fellow-princes, finds it difficult to adjust himself to the changed political order. He recollects with nostalgia the sweet days of the British Raj.

Bawajiraj III in *The Golden Honeycomb* is educated by English tutors to suit to the Britishers' purpose :

> There is his upbringing. As heir to the throne, he has gone, barely touching common soil, from the hands of his assiduous tutor for the sons of princes and noblemen founded on British principles and initiative and intended to function as an Indian Eton (33).

He is admitted into the Military Academy which is administered by the British officials. Then he undergoes training in civil administration which is a privilege for the aristocratic class. Bawajiraj's schooling has enabled him to establish friendship with the English. Indeed, he is most ardently at home with them, he feels he is one of them. It is through such Indian princes that the British were engaged, as Susheela N. Rao says, 'in a complex web of intrigues and counter-intrigues' (8). Acting as intermediary between the emperor and the subjects, the Indian rulers have no choice but to serve British interests.

In *A Silence of Desire*, Dandekar with his Western attitude to life is set against the spiritual minded Sarojini. It is a study of the urban lower middle-class domestic life where ideological conflicts lead to serious problems of inter-personal communication. Dandekar is modern, educated and Westernized. As G. Nageswar Rao observes, 'He is a typical example of an ordinary educated Indian whose response to everything in life is illustrative of western influence on a sensibility based and nourished on Indian philosophical heritage' (165). Dandekar's Westernized views, his skeptical attitude towards traditional faith make him oppose Sarojini's convictions of faith cure. But Dandekar is not wholly western. He believes in the traditional concept of a Hindu wife's devotion and absolute loyalty to her husband. Eventually, it is Sarojini who succeeds in bringing round Dandekar to her fold rather than Dandekar being able to pursuade his wife for medical treatment. He is made free from his narrow and negative outlook, obsessions and unfounded suspicions about the Swamy. He is finally convinced that the Swamy as a spiritual guide is significant for the suffering humanity. Anita Mahajan rightly comments :

> The world of *A Silence of Desire* is the world of science and superstition carefully balanced. Kamala Markandaya's attitude is that of reconciliation between the two, science must co-exist with human faith (144).

The process of modernization has been most succinctly embodied in the character of Laxman in *The Nowhere Man.* His father, Srinivas, is a long-time migrant from India who lives in London. But his mother Vasantha, never accepts England as her home. Born in London Laxman grows up into an independent young boy strongly influenced by western education. Contrary to the parents' desire he joins war. While working in an engineering firm, he is engaged to a Christian girl named Pat, whom he eventually marries without the knowledge and consent of the parents. He appears 'a pale brown Englishman with a pale pink wife' (33). He lives away from his parents and is totally indifferent to their well-being. He shifts the responsibility of his ailing mother to the National Health Care. Vasantha hopes to come back to her country after her recovery from tuberculosis. When she dies, Laxman does not attend the funeral on the plea that he suffers from influenza. It is Srinivas who performs the rituals and fulfils her last wishes to sprinkle Indian soil and Ganges water on her dead body. Being totally integrated into the Western culture, Laxman gives no value to familial sentiments. Brought up in the western ethos, his outlook is absolutely materialistic and commercial. His visits to his lonely and suffering father is only casual and formal. He contemptuously calls his father's living place 'a pigsty.' When he comes to learn about his father contracting leprosy, he is outraged, "Coming to a country, he said to himself, doing his best to offend it. Sticking out like a sore thumb, instead of decently integrating..... Crowning it all by contracting of all things, this medieval disease" (261). But despite Laxman's attempts to assimilate himself with the British community, there lurks within him a serious identity crisis. He is shocked to find that though coloured people fight and die for England like his brother Seshu they are treated as aliens. Like his father he strives for racial harmony but is always confused and bewildered. Though a British citizen by birth, Laxman is forced, ironically, to defend himself and his father against racial discrimination. Srinivas' lonely suffering is not merely due to death of Vasantha and Seshu but due to the racist attitude of the English community and the callousness and neglect of his son Laxman. Finally, when he comes to support and save his father from the fire, it is too late. Thus, both the father and the son become victims of racial rancour which turns them into nowhere men.

In *Two Virgins* the impact of westernisation is clearly evinced in the character of Lalitha. It is Appa, her father who encourages her to be western-oriented. He wishes his daughter to be educated in the city and move in high class society. Aunt Alamelu questions the justification of teaching Christian ways to the Hindu maidens. She is convinced that Miss Mendoza, the Head Mistress of the Christian Missionary school Lalitha attends, has come to the village to spoil the native traditions and young girls like Lalitha. Miss Mendoza and Mr. Gupta represent the corrupting influence of Western culture on India. Margaret P. Joseph says :

> Miss Mendoza the teacher and Mr. Gupta the film director are instrumental in taking Lalitha away from her family. They are utilized structurally in the text to enlarge on the vicious results of western influence. Both of them have been trained abroad, and the injection of alien fashions like high heeled shoes, and cream silk suits into the village setting, rouse Lalitha's mother and aunt to vehement denunciation of such life style (83).

The strong and deep-rooted cultural basis of Amma and Aunt Alamelu militates against such corrupting influences. They condemn the glamorous city life as western punk which actually shatters their domestic bliss. Even Lalitha's younger sister Saroja is immensely disturbed by the western encroachment into their sweet family life. In their Deepavali celebration the whole family misses Lalitha as she has been taken to the city for her training as an actress. Under Western impact the Hindu joint family has received a strong jolt. Saroja becomes aware of the predicament of modernization from her sister's example. She clings to her native tradition. While Lalitha is prone to western influences, Saroja is quite happy and content in the old established mode of village life. Alice Drum remarks :

> By having Saroja voice this message Markandaya sides with many Third World writers who stress the importance of a nation's maintaining its own cultural identity, dancing its own dances, in the face of encroaching westernisation (327).

But the novel is suggestive of the author's resignation to the inevitable path of the future of India. It implies that in spite of the vehement opposition of the older generation, the traditionalists, the country is bound to proceed towards industrialization and Westernisation.

In *The Coffer Dams* the relationship between Clinton and the native workers is that of a master and a slave. The impersonality of western technology is set against the innocence and warmth of the aborigines. Clinton is disdainful of the natives. He never calls them by their names. He brushes them off like flies. He is never concerned about their problems. He has no human feelings for the workers who dies in accidents. The Indian labourers are victimized by the commercial minded English technocrats. The coffer dams are completed at the cost of human lives. Clinton in fact, represents the die hard British attitude of aggressiveness towards the colonized.

In *The Nowhere Man,* radicals like Fred Fletcher, Mike, Bill and Joe react strongly against the coloured immigrants. Even though in Srinivas there is absolutely no hatred for the Britishers, no sense of bitterness towards his neighbours, Fred and Mrs. Glass, he is constantly ill-treated by this hostile group. Fred, a frustrated young man, experiencing failure and defeat everywhere blames the immigrant Indians for problems of unemployment, congestion and unhygienic conditions. He nourishes anger and hatred for the coloured ones, 'He decided he hated that colour, and the untold evils he and his kind were letting loose in his country….' (165). Fred's so-called patriotism is scoffed at when he leaves his beloved England for Australia in search of job. But such animosity leads him nowhere. In a fit of rage he lits fire which goes beyond his control. So finally, the hater meets a suffocating death along with the victim.

Against these Britishers who are avowedly anti-Indians, Markandaya presents a few Britishers who are compassionate and loving towards suffering Indians. Dr. Radcliffe, Mrs. Pickering and Mrs. Fletcher represent this group who love India and Indians. Dr. Radcliffe is anguished at the growing animosity, intolerance, suspicion and jealously in the minds of the so called civilized people against the coloured immigrants. He believes that Srinivas dies not due to fire but out of shock. It is the racial prejudice and the inhumanity that hastens his death. Dr. Radcliffe is quite at home with the leprosy patients. He comes across during his stint of work in India. In England though he does not treat such patients, he helps them to got to the hospital for Tropical diseases. He gives Srinivas hope that it is not incurable. He goes to the extent of neglecting his own comforts and pleasure for the sake of his patients. His wife gets intolerant when she finds the doctor busy with 'those dreadful patients' (11). Srinivas is impressed by his 'professional gentleness which he brought to patients he knew to be sick and beyond his skill to cure' (15). After the final tragedy the doctor blames himself for his inability to prevent the inhuman dogma of racial hatred.

Mrs. Pickering appears in the life of Srinivas when he is in an acute state of desperation and loneliness. She takes care of his household. Together they argue on matters of war, peace, nationality, politics, racism, Eastern and Western traditions and cultures. She is aggrieved at the suffering of coloured people in her country. She warns Srinivas not to go out as she apprehends physical assault on him. She tries to comfort him with consoling words, through she is sure of the inevitable disaster that would befall Srinivas. Like Dr. Radcliffe she blames her own people and her inability to resist the final tragedy of Srinivas' death by fire.

Like Mrs. Pickering, Mrs. Fletcher also behaves as a true Christian, a good neighbour to Srinivas. She is a sympathetic, reasonable and strong willed English woman. She always warns her erring son Fred against ill feeling for the coloured people. She is moved to see Srinivas praying for the departed soul of her husband at the time of his death. She tries to convince Mrs. Glass and other neighbours that the Asians are no danger to their life. She accepts him as a good neighbour and assures him, 'you've as much right to be here as any of us and there's few as wouldn't be sorry if you were to feel you had to leave because of what our Fred said' (166). She insists Fred to apologize whenever he disgraces or ill-treats the old Srinivas.

Like Mrs. Pickering, Mrs. Fletcher, Helen in *The Coffer Dams* has been portrayed as an ardent supporter of the Indians. If her husband, Clinton is aspirant of personal glory and commercial benefits for his own country, Helen goes on defending the natives' rights. If Clinton considers everything from the point of view of technical skill and material gains, Helen has a humanitarian attitude towards life. She strives to understand the problems of the common folk and improve their life style. She tries to learn their language to understand them better. She argues vehemently with Clinton on the issue of the natives' removal from their habitation for the Britishers' accommodation. Reacting to the killing of two labourers by the machine, Helen says in an ironic tone, 'It is not the dying,' she said, 'Lives have been lost before. They are used to death, it is every day and they see it, having no hospitals to cover up' (177). Helen suspects Clinton to be the cause of Bashiam's accident. She rushes to the injured Bashiam and tries her best to console him and prays for his speedy recovery, while Clinton is cool and indifferent. Helen clearly perceives the feeling of social and economic compulsion with which the natives tend to accept the change, 'A backward people, whose primeval ways had exasperated successive governments, monumental impediments in the path of progressive companies and administrations, even they had felt the glancing blow of social change' (72). Thus, from the beginning to the end Helen keeps up her spirit of compassion and love for the poor Indian workers.

Dr. Keny, the British philanthropist, chooses Indian village as his place for missionary work. As the narrative moves from Rukmani's girlhood to her maturing into a mother and grandmother, Dr. Kenny remains a benefactor and source of help and solace to her. Rukmani realizes that despite being alien, people like Dr. Kenny are basically human and compassionate, 'Have I not so much sense to see that you are not one of us? You live and work here, and there is in your heart solicitude for us and love for our children' (111). Kenny's response to this reveals the humanity in him, 'Because they have learnt of your need. Do not the sick die in the streets because there is no hospital for them?' (115). Kenny feels that it is the moral responsibility of the British to take care of the well-being of the backward people. He is worried about the Indian sense of fatalism, submission to passive suffering and resignation to adversity. He reacts strongly when he sees Rukmani starving with her family, 'You meek suffering fools. Why do you keep this ghastly silence? Why do you not demand, cry out for help — do something?' (47-48).

However, Nathan and Rukmani ideologically differ from Kenny's materialistic approach. The way the poor Indian peasants survive the tremendous hardships of life is beyond the understanding of the western rationalists. The younger generation, however, learn to accept the change from an agrarian to an industrial social order. Rukmani's son Selvam is absorbed in Kenny's hospital and ironically Rukmani takes her final retreat in Selvam's place offered to him by the generous Kenny. The hospital is the uniting force. Ira's albino child is accepted here. Puli's leprosy is treated here with compassion. Kenny tries to enlighten the ignorant villagers, 'you must cry out if you want help. It is no use whatsoever to suffer in silence' (115). Thus, two distinct cultures-the old world of faith and the new world of science are integrated and reconciled by the cultivation of mutual trust, co-operation and understanding.

The possibility of such mutual cooperation and understanding is more obviously reflected in Kamala Markandaya's last novel *Pleasure City*. As in *The Coffer Dams,* here also the ancient traditions of an isolated little fishing village in India have been threatened by modern technology. The British construction company brings tremendous change in the fishing community. The native fishermen get inspired by the improved techniques offered to them by the British. Tully stands for the liberal British capitalists. He befriends Rikki, the fishing boy who is assured for an alluring job in the project "Shalimar". Tully is kind and considerate. He readily accepts the orphan boy Rikki who is already sheltered and educated in the school of the Bridies, the English missionary couple. Rikki soon abandons his traditional profession of fishing and takes to building yacht. He is now free from material worries as he earns a steady income provided by Tully. When after completion of the project, Tully leaves for England, Rikki is overwhelmed with grief. He comes back to his family and ancestral profession, with an enlightened mind. Tully too returns to his country with the feeling of a strong bond with the native Indians. Thus, Tully and Rikki part from each other with a sense of harmony and peaceful co-existence.

In *Some Inner Fury,* Kamala Markandaya has delineated characters among the educated Indians having three distinct attitudes towards the West. There are people like Kit and his father who owe allegiance towards the West and the British government as they hold high position in the British government in India. Western culture has entered deep into their blood. Roshan and Mira belong to the second category of people who are educated in Western fashion but are deeply concerned with the freedom of the country. Govind belongs to the third category of people who are tradition bound, hostile towards the British rule in India and are prepared to overthrow the government by all means including violence.

Mira is brought up in a rich, sophisticated family that prides itself in being a part of the British social circle. In spite of her mother's warnings she engages herself with Richard, the Britisher, in pre-marital relationship. She goes to the club to socialize with the Europeans. Despite such social habits, Mira soon realizes that the British are here to exploit and to oppress. When she prepares a report on a British sponsored project, she is quite seeptic about the government's sincerity in implementing any welfare project for the Indians. She completely loses confidence on the Britishers when she listens to the British magistrate's prejudiced judgement in the trial of Govind. It is this realization that impels her to reject Richard who belongs to the class of oppressors.

Though Roshan Merchant, the journalist, is a close associate of Mira, she is a westernized woman, educated in Oxford, who comes back to India and chooses to work for the uplift of the Indians. Her weekly articles expose the British atrocities on the poor, weak, innocent and ignorant Indians. She joins the national agitation conducted by Govind and pleads for boycotting foreign goods. She stops smoking and using lipstick. She throws her foreign garments and uses homespun ones. She travels in train as a mark of civil disobedience for which her paper is proscribed. Yet her spirit remains indomitable. Like the two great English reformists, sister Nivedita and Annie Besant, Roshan works for the Indian causes. Though westernized, she exemplifies her patriotic and nationalistic bent of mind.

In clear contrast to Kit, Govind expresses his strong apathy towards the foreign rulers. Out of his extreme patriotic fervour, he uses violence, with a view to getting freedom for his country. He is full of sympathy and affection for Premala who is neglected in Kit's household and who is the symbol of service, sacrifice and non-violence. Govind is full of hatred for the missionary. He opposes and despises the missionaries 'who not only set up their alien and unwanted institutions in the land but who, for the preservation of these institutions, invariably sided with those other white men who ruled the country' (166). Finally, it is Premala who is actively engaged in such an institution of the missionary Hicky and who is victimized in the conflict leading to her tragic end. Such is the fatal consequence of the racial bitterness existing between Hicky and Govind. Not only is the school set on fire killing Premala, but also hatred and wrath and vengeance bring about an abrupt and violent end to Kit's life as well. Govind is accused of murder but the nationalists are successful in bailing him out of the accusation. Mira supports her brother at the cost of her love for Richard. She is jubilant over the freedom of Govind while being fully conscious of her heart weeping 'tearless, desolate, silently to itself' (285).

In *The Golden Honeycomb* Rabindranath is portrayed as a great nationalist. He opposes his father supporting the British political agent at the cost of the subjects of the state. His patriotic feelings create awakening among the masses. With the help of his mother and grandmother, he violates the royal tradition of getting education in the Military Academy. From his state wide tour he gets enlightened about the suffering of the people. He forsakes the rich splendour and luxury of the princely life style. Rabi being the heir apparent takes upon himself the task of bridging the gap between the ruler and the ruled. From his young age he develops friendship with both Sophie, the Resident's charming daughter and Janaki, the sweeper girl. His mental make up has been moulded on the great national heroes of the past. He has been taught to feel proud of his own culture, belonging to his own people. On the brink of adulthood, when he experiences reality outside the palace, he identifies himself with the common men suffering in poverty and hunger. The Mill workers' strike in Bombay enlightens him about injustice to the poor labourers. He is seriously upset by his father's act of importing costly Rolls-Royces and living in luxurious hotels in Bombay, in total indifference towards the suffering common men.

Rabi learns his life's lesson from the experience of his stay with the workers. He promises to raise their standard of living when he would be the ruler of the state. People rush to him with their native problems, and start agitation against undue levies and taxes thrust on common men. Maharajah is annoyed at Rabi's behaviours. When he accuses his son of damaging the state, Rabi replies, "We rajahs and nawabs have rent the country apart for a century and more and in the process traders and soldiers of fortune have been elevated into emperors. The people are attempting to repair the damage" (416). Rabi is sure that the working class and the lower class cannot raise their voice against the cruel rulers as they belong to 'A race that would always be defeated' (462).

The inter-cultural encounters thus throw up a variety of men and women, both Indian and British, who have varying attitudes of mutual love and hatred, concern and indifference. While loyalists of the west, among whom are both the Britishers and the so-called Indian elite, tend to subvert the nationalist aspirations, there are also highly sensitive men and women of both the nationalities who swear by the human values of compassion and freedom. As Ramesh Chadha observes :

> She examines the strengths and weaknesses of both the cultures. In extolling the philosophical and religious attitude of the Indian people and their spiritual strength, she is not uncritical of their economic backwardness, their superstitious nature, their abject poverty, squalor, ignorance, illiteracy, fatalism and passive endurance, nor does she underestimate the contribution of the west, especially that of Britain, as patron and mentor, its missionary zeal, its scientific and technological advancement, its rationalism and liberal outlook (Cross-cultural, 1988, 144).

V

Markandays's perception of Indian life, in short, constitutes a social order that has created a new form of class-hierarchy : the factory-owner and the wage-earner, the elite class and the illiterate, the skilled trader and the traditional shop-keeper, people aspiring for urban comforts and those clinging to conventional cultural practices. In other words, the incoming of technology has resulted in a clear rural-urban divide leading to a duality of classes — the haves and the have-nots, the exploiter and the exploited.

4

Markandaya, Class-consciousness and Other Voices

Since class-consciousness is an essential component of the Indian psyche, it is but imperative that any fiction built on Indian life and society will have to foreground this consciousness in order to be credible and significant. A study of the major works by Mulk Raj Anand, Bhabani Bhattacharya, Raja Rao, Arun Joshi, Anita Desai, and Ruth Prawar Jhabvala would show that though Kamala Markandaya's perception of Indian ethos is strikingly similar to that of these novelists, there is, nevertheless, a unique sensitiveness in her novels in terms of the extent, range and depth of perception.

The novelists of the pre-Independence era were influenced by Gandhian ideology and tried to create literature of social concern. The general trend of social concern of the thirties and forties finds clear reflection in the works of K.S. Venkataramani, Raja Rao, Bhabani Bhattacharya and Mulk Raj Anand. These novelists chose themes and characters with distinct class-identities. If Tagore shows his interest in the upper classes and the middle classes and Sarat Chatterjee in the lower middle classes, Mulk Raj Anand is concerned with the proletariat. Through the pen-portraits of the untouchable sweepers, the labourers, the house-hold servants, the coolies and the landless farmers, Mulk Raj Anand exposes cruelty and harassment to the downtrodden. Like Orwell and Maxim Gorky, he has deep sympathy for the destitute and the underprivileged. He attacks the caste and class-systems in India. He upholds the rights of the mine workers, the factory workers, the land labourers and daily wage earners. Both Mulk Raj Anand and Kamala Markandaya are concerned with the poverty and hunger of the working class. The theme of hunger is the basic focus in Anand's *Coolie*, *The Old Woman* and *The Road* as well as in Markandaya's *Nectar in a Sieve*, and *A Handful of Rice.* There is a general view of the gloomy picture of the exodus from the village to the city. There are common scenes of the famished, the underfed hungry masses struggling for a morsel of food. The arrogance and inhumanity of the rich and the privileged have been condemned in the same tone as the servility and docility of the labourers.

Anand's early novels present a reflection of actual life lived by the less fortunate, the lowly and the disinherited. *Untouchable* is a story of a young sweeper boy, Bakha who belongs to the lowest rung in the social strata. *Coolie* is a proletarian tragedy of an orphan boy, Munoo who passes through diverse situations — as a domestic servant in an urban middle-class family in Sham Nagar, as a worker in a small pickle factory in Daulatpur, as a labourer in a cotton mill in Bombay and as a rickshaw puller in Simla. His father's land is seized by the money-lender, leading to his 'slow death of bitterness and disappointment' (11). His mother soon dies in poverty. The boy's right to life is most brutally and tragically denied to him. As a servant, he is not allowed to play with the children of the master. In the bank sub-Accountant Babu Nathoo Ram's house he is warned, "You are a servant, you must not play with us" (45). But the innocent boy does not know the barriers between classes. When he playfully bites Sheikha, the master's daughter, he is savagely beaten up. He is forced into the life of a beast of burden, carrying heavy loads to earn his livelihood. With the help of the elephant driver he goes to Bombay. He sleeps with the pavement dwellers. He is soon disgusted with the intolerable conditions of the factory workers in Sir George White Cotton Mills. In Munoo there is deep-rooted feeling of inferiority as he watches people who live in bungalows and wear *Angrezi* clothes. The English people have an impression of the Indian poor as dirty and diseased, and so they deal with them contemptuously. K.V. Reddy aptly observes, '*Coolie* is a sincere protest against the emergence of a new world of money and exploitation and class distinction' (12). When Munoo goes to Simla and works as a rickshaw puller of Mrs. Mainswaring, he is hard pressed and dies of consumption at a tender age of sixteen. Thus the merciless, mechanical rhythm of urban life into which the innocent poor rustic boy is thrust, churns him into death. He realizes the truth, "The bigger the city is the more cruel it is" (177).

Kamala Markandaya has presented similar conditions of the Indian villagers in *Nectar in a Sieve*, *Possession* and *A Handful of Rice.* Like Munoo, Val leaves his native place under economic pressure. He gets the news of his mother's death when he is engrossed in his prospective career-making endeavours. In *A Handful of Rice* Ravi goes to city leaving behind his native land and his parents. But he is disillusioned and disappointed when all his attempts to over come hunger, debt and economic insecurity turn futile. In his own village, his father has to endure poverty due to the corrupt money-lenders , the black marketeers, and the defective land and food distribution systems. It is in the city that Ravi observes the big gap between the rich and the poor :

> The cost of just one of those motor-cars that purred along the marina, he felt, would keep him and his family over half a life time. How, he wondered with a burning curiosity, did any one ever earn so much? He never would, not if he sewed a dozen shirts in a dozen hours every day of the week for a dozen years (134).

In the same way, Munoo starts for the city with dreams of wonderful things people speak of the babus, the sahibs, their silk clothes, and delicacies. But when he enters the town he notices some people carrying loads of luggage on their backs. The grand marble buildings surprise him. He is disturbed by Master Nathoo Ram wearing black shoes while his own feet lie bare. He realizes the contrast between his own starved life and the master and his children wearing silk clothes, warm woolen suit and eating sweetmeat. He broods over his inferior status when he sees his master using modern amenities like shaving razor, radio set, musical instruments and various machineries. Bibiji, the wife of Babu Nathoo Ram, humiliates him and condemns him when he laughs. 'What right has he to join the laughter of his superiors?' (31). The hotel boy treats him like an untouchable. He is shocked to find himself misfit and unwanted in the rich man's world. He accepts his inferior position in society as a slave but observes, 'There must be two kinds of people in the world, the rich and the poor' (69). The rich merchants in starched muslims stand contrasted to the dark coolies in patched up rags. The impressive bungalows of the English residents look down upon the congested hovels of the coolies.

Kamala Markandaya creates a similar situation in *The Coffer Dams*. The company people from England occupy the tribal lands, live luxuriously, seducing them by low wages, bribes and temporary jobs. The technological appliances run by the workers' sweat bring profit to the employees, but death and damage to the workers. In *Nectar in a Sieve* Kamala Markandaya depicts the bitter experiences of Nathan and Rukmani in the city. When they approach the Collector's residence and the Doctor's residence, they are driven out as beggars and servants. They are not allowed to use the main-gate at the front of the bungalows. Munoo is similarly forbidden in the master's house to play with children. This creates utter dejection in the child's mind. At the end of the novel Munoo, like Nathan, dies fatigued and consumptive, of hard work in frail physique.

Both Anand and Markandaya show that humanity is not completely lost. Fellow-feeling, a sense of compassion still exists. In *Nectar in a Sieve* food is distributed in the temple. Rukmani rushes to the spot and gets food for both herself and the old man. In *Two Virgins* the author narrates the scene of poor people given food once a day in the temple arena by the priests. Mulk Raj Anand also points out how human charity is displayed at the shrine of Har Dayal and free food is distributed to the mendicants and the starving ones. Munoo, though a child, reflects, 'Why are some men so good and others bad, some like Prabha and the elephant driver, others like Ganpat and the policemen who beat me at the railway station?' (171).

Prabha, the partner in Ganpat's industrial enterprise is portrayed as a noble character, like Dr. Radcliffe in *The Nowher Man,* who has sympathy for the poor and the weaker sections of society. Sauda the labour leader works like Kenny for justice to the workers. As Kenny tries to convince Rukmani and the villagers of their rights, Sauda makes the workers aware of their miserable condition. Like Rukmani, Munoo also accepts suffering. There is a common feeling, "We belong to suffering, we belong to suffering" (247). The striking coolies are weak, filthy and spineless. Sauda explains to them about their own status :

> "We are human beings and not soul-less machines."
> "We want the right to work without having to pay bribes."
> "We want clean houses to live in."
> "We want to be saved from the clutches of the money-lenders."
> "We want a good wage" (267).

Such inspiring words excite and strengthen the mind of the coolies. They realize that they are deprived of fundamental freedom. They are over-worked and under-paid. About the master's repression and callous attitude Sauda explains, "The rich and the powerful, the magnificent and the glorious, whose opulence is built on robbery and theft and open warfare, are honoured and admired by the whole world" (266). But the humble workers are wretchedly swindled out of their rights. They are respected by none.

In *Two Leaves and a Bud* Mulk Raj Anand dramatizes the tragic clash between indifferent and cruel masters and the Tea plantation coolies. Gangu like Munoo wants to work and to live. Both are victims of capitalism and exploitation. The rich eat and drink and play while the poor labourers are underpaid, underfed and over-worked. Like Sauda, de la Havre, the humanist and social critic consoles and encourages the ignorant and dismayed coolies and inspires them to fight against abysmal poverty, stark cruelty and the dark social forces.

Kamala Markandaya's Ravi in *A Handful of Rice* resents stitching aprons as he feels exploited by the Eve Shopkeeper who pays him eighty rupees per dozen as stitching charges whereas the shopkeeper himself gets from customers one hundred and twentyfive rupees per piece. Apu has patiently tolerated the injustice, but the youngman Ravi is enraged with impotent fury against the rich and reacts violently. The novel ends with a note of passive resignation as he cannot accept and act in the hooligan Damodar's world of crime and violence.

Anand's trilogy *The Village* deals with the impingement of industrialization on the old order of rural society and the decline of the peasantry as a self-reliant class. The landlord system has been vehemently denounced. The Britishers are condemned as the agents of exploitation. Lal Sing, the youngest son of a peasant family in Nandpur reacts sharply against the injustices the simple rural folk have to put up with. Lalu's suffering at the hands of the landlord Harban Singh, the money lender Seth Chaman Lal, the Sikh priest and his own conservative family provoke angry revolutionary sentiments within him. He is disgusted with the religious orthodoxy of the society for which he feels people cannot progress. He tries to make the tenant farmers aware of their position and unite them against their exploiters. The death of Ravi's son in *A Handful of Rice* impels his to join the revolutionary movement for a handful of rice but the birth of Lalu's son symbolizes the rise of a new generation with the hope of freedom and prosperity.

Bhabani Bhattacharya, too, reflects his deep concern at the state of poverty and exploitation in the Indian society. All the novels of Bhattacharya are in fact built on the theme of contrast between the rich and the poor. In *So Many Hungers (1947)* Bhattacharya shows that the famine of 1942 in Bengal was caused by faulty social systems. Samarendra Basu with his two sons constitutes a well-to-do family. The father being an influential man takes advantage of the fluctuating stock market and starts hoarding grains, while the villagers being misguided by the government agents sell all their rice. It results in artificial scarcity and man-made famine. Millions of people die of hunger. The poor, ignorant and uneducated peasants consider it to be 'their fate, as expiation of sins of past lives' (108). There is a similar reference to the rural people's sense of fatalism in Kamala Markandaya's *Nectar in a Sieve*. Rukmani in a mood of self-assessment speaks to Kenny, "Yet our priests fast, and inflict on themselves severe punishments, and we are taught to bear our sorrows in silence, and all this is so that the soul may be cleansed" (116).

In *So many Hungers* there are distressing scenes of the starving and dying people. Children are sold. Girls are allowed to take to prostitution. Kajoli with her mother and brother comes to the city and lives on begging. When it is difficult to manage living with only begging, she thinks of selling her body, but fortunately she finds a path of earning by selling newspaper. In *Nectar in a Sieve* there are harrowing scenes of wide-spread hunger. Kamala Markandaya shows that the misery of poor peasants is caused by nature's ravages and human crookedness, but Bhattacharya fixes responsibility on the anti-social cruel traders who create artificial storage of food. He severely condemns the dehumanized rich people. Like Ira, Kajoli cannot stand the misery of the starving family, but unlike Ira who takes to prostitution and is abused by her father, Kajoli refrains from the heinous profession.

Bhattacharya's *He Who Rides A Tiger* (1952) presents the character of a village blacksmith, Kalo. Poverty, unemployment, decay of cottage industries drive him from his village Jharna to the city. While stealing bananas to satisfy his hunger he is imprisoned. Coming out of prison he works in a brothel and coincidentally finds his daughter there. Kalo takes revenge on the rich class and the upper caste people like Abalabandhu, by acting as a Brahmin priest and distributing their donation of milk for lord Shiva to the poor hungry babies, for he knows the pangs of hunger. Thus the novel is a grim satire on the Hindu orthodoxy. The suppressed awareness of his low birth turns him into a rebel, waging war against an unjust social system. The novel champions the cause of the down-trodden and condemns cruelty of the rich merchants and the hoarders. There is a heart-rending narration of the procession of the poor and the hungry demanding food-grains from the rich people. Weavers sell their looms, artisans their tools, fishermen their boats just as Nathan and Rukmani sell their utensils, clothes and other essentials to make their both ends meet. There is cry from the aggrieved mass of hungry people, 'Food! Food! Food! for the hungry. The cry filled the air of the great city' (167).

In *A Handful of Rice* Kamala Markandaya has narrated a similar scene of a hungry procession. Ravi joins the procession proceeding towards the rice godown with cries of protest against injustice and inequality :

> Ravi felt the force, he could feel himself being sucked into it, but part of him was still benumbed, he could not quicken as a young man would, he could not manage the act of surrender. But he went with them marching alongside students and workmen, and petty craftsmen like himself with the same fires burning their bellies (233).

The rich tradesmen and merchants are shocked by the agitated commoners' demand for rice.

In *A Goddess Named Gold* (1960), Bhattacharya attacks the rich tradesmen and shopkeepers for their exploitation of the masses. The avaricious instincts of Seth Samsundar has been condemned. He is a proud, greedy cloth merchant. Mira is an uneducated village girl who launches a successful campaign against the Seth who is forced to sell cloth at fair price. She explains to the women about their position in society and the values of changing times. She sees the co-existence of riches and poverty, paupers and millionaires as light and darkness. Laxmi, the Seth's wife represents the modern resurgent women who fight for their rights and against social injustice. She does not hesitate to lead the village women in their march even against her husband.

Raja Rao also deals with social issues like poverty, untouchability, illiteracy, backwardness, superstition, widowhood and dowry in his first novel *Kanthapura* (1938). The context of *Kanthapura* is the Freedom Movement. The villagers do not understand Gandhi's philosophy but they are aware of the values in the struggle for independence. Raja Rao is primarily concerned with the poor, the workers, the untouchables and the destitutes. In the framework of non-violent, non-co-operation movement of the twenties the story gives an insight into the appalling social conditions of the village and the values that help people to withstand the agonies of flood, famine, fire and exploitation. In the small village Kanthapura, the most important event is the ploughing of the field at the first rains. This village soon turns into a center of national activities. The village consists of Brahmin quarters, the Sudra quarters and the pariah quarters. This caste structure of the village is an age-old tradition splitting the inhabitants into group identities. Among the rich class are Patel Range Gowda who has built a nine beamed house and has procured gold, and Bhatta, the Zamindar, who has amassed wet lands of the peasants. The extended house of Patwari Nanjundiah shows his high financial and social status. The village Post-Master Suryanarayan having a two-storied building leads a comfortable middle-class life. In contrast to this privileged class, there are poor people who are badly dressed, are homeless, and cannot pay the tax of the land. Just beyond the village lies the Skeffington Coffee Estate, symbolizing the intrusion of industrialization and westernisation into the traditional agrarian community.

Being inspired by Gandhi's ideology, a Brahmin youngman, Moorthy devotes himself to the task of educating the pariahs. Ratna, a young widow joins him defying traditional restrictions on her. The weavers, the potters, the pariahs, even 'the blue, pot-bellied, half-nacked coolies' (147) from the Coffee Estate join them in their resistance to exploitation. Moorthy preaches them brotherhood, equality, castelessness and abolition of untouchability. He is not an intellectual but an idealist who tries to rouse the village from its slumber and complacency. Raja Rao delineates the atrocities of the British police on the coolies of the Coffee Estate. Raja Rao's coolies have the same fate as Mulk Raj Anand's. They are described as half-necked, starving, diseased with bundles of essentials as their sole possession. They work with the Red Master, brutally humiliated. They tolerate their humiliations, sickness and violation of their women's honour.

Kamala Markandaya has presented a similar life pattern of the workers in *The Coffer Dams*. Krishnan, the Indian Engineer in Clinton's Company speaks of the savage tribal as those used to being done out of their rights. Helen is shocked at the emotional cauldron that Britain the ruler and India the ruled have kept on the boil throughout the terms of an imposed over-lordship. When Helen explains to the tribal chief about the benefit they will receive after the work is done and the British Company goes back, the old man is sceptical, '...they will learn what is real and mourn what is lost. A score or more before they bend the river.... The Great Dam will take them, the man-eater will have its flesh' (73). From among the tribal, Bashiam has been selected and detribalized as he is skilled and competent technician. The death of the Chief suggests that individual life and property has to be sacrificed to achieve material progress.

The coolies in The Skeffington Coffee Estate have been appointed to help the Britishers in plantation activities. They grow sick in unhealthy atmosphere. They spend all their earning in drinking toddy. Kamala Markandaya in her *Possession* describes similar condition of the impoverished peasant with 'under-nourished bellies' (10). Moorthy becomes the flag bearer of the movement of liberation and prohibition. The coolies being aware of their misery join the procession. With the villagers they start picketing at toddy booths. They prefer suffering, banishment, even death to submission to atrocities. The novel ends with the total destruction of the village. Inspite of the look of desolation the village Kanthapura achieves the glory of bringing about a zest for reformation and social and political awareness among the rural poor. Thus, in *Kanthapura* as Srinivasa Iyengar says :

> A village, a picturesque region, an epoch of social and political change, a whole complex of character and motive, reason and superstition, idealism and cold calculation, all spring up before our eyes demanding recognition and acceptance; it is almost a tour de force (392).

In Arun Joshi's *The Foreigner* (1968) Sindi Oberoi suffers from rootlessness and loneliness. He does not belong to any country or culture. As he does not marry June, his American girl friend, Babu Khemka, the son of a wealthy Indian businessman comes forward and marries her. When June asks whether doughnuts are available in India, Babu says 'Only upper class Indians do.' When June asks why they are so expensive, Babu replies, 'No, they are not expensive. But the lower class people are just not progressive' (93). This shows the Indian upper class attitude towards the lower class. Babu is, in fact, encouraged by his parents to go to America for higher studies, to learn modern methods of technology and establish himself in sophisticated and progressive society. But after coming in contact with American life-style, he has destroyed his roots and native culture. Oberoi admits about his predicament of rootless existence when he speaks to Babu, 'You had a clear-cut system of morality, a caste system that laid down all you had to do. You had a God, you had roots in the soil you lived upon. Look at me. I have no roots, I have no system of morality' (135-136).

In contrast to Oberoi, Babu has factories and industrial set up and financial stability to come back to. Yet bad influence of the Western culture has hastened his premature sad demise. Srinivas, in Markandaya's *The Nowhere Man* even after long stay in London does not find any strong support in moments of extreme despair. He leaves his country, his fellowmen, his friends and relatives. Gradually his wife and sons leave him through death and separation. Towards the end of his life, he suffers from a sense of restlessness out of his unaccommodated alien conditions. In spite of the mental and spiritual help extended to him by Dr. Radcliffe and Mrs. Pickering, Srinivas is victimized by racial violence.

Kamala Markandaya envisages in Laxman a new dimension of the problem of identity. However, engrossed and integrated in the western life pattern, he feels utterly lost. He tenaciously wishes to belong to the country in which he was born, and lived and laboured, not in some reservation rusted up within it. Towards the end of the novel, he is left alone to suffer through his precarious condition of a '*Nowhere Man,*' having lost all his past, his blood relations and the contact of the cultural heritage. He has to encounter his existential problem attenuated by an identity crisis. Like Arun Joshi, Kamala Markandaya has also depicted modern man's predicament consequent upon his alienation, rootlessness and misadjustment in an alien surrounding.

In *The Strange Case of Billy Biswas* (1971) Arun Joshi presents in Billy the portrait of a foreigner who cannot identify himself with the society of which he is a product. Coming back learned from America, he leaves the so-called civilized world of greed, rivalry, anxiety and hypocrisy. He disappears into the forest of the Maikala Hills. In the forest he finds no concern with price, technology, electron and all commercial business so typical of a degenerated society. He feels only the earth, trees, rain, dust storm, river, animals, birds, free love and sex. He loves the tribal girl Bilasia, the essence of the primitive force he was searching for. The civilized world calls him a rebel but the tribals worship him as their God. He tells Dunia, the Tribal chief, "I am fed up of those slimy bastards who are camped across the river, and I am fed up of the millions who surround me in the wretched city where I come from" (144). He takes refuge in the tribal land revolting against the social norms for which he has been penalized with death. The author exposes such life of discontent in modern men like Sind Oberoi, Billy Biswas, Ratan in *Apprentice* (1981) and Som Bhaskar in *The Last Labyrinth* (1981). Amidst wealth, power, privilege and enlightenment, these men suffer emotionally because they lack the deeper equilibrium of the spirit.

In *The Coffer Dams* Kamala Markandaya shows in Helen similar hankering for an association with nature and men of nature. Dissociating herself from her civilized husband Clinton, she escapes into the tribal abode of flora and fauna. Like Billy Biswas she is sympathetic to the poor, the ignorant tribals who sacrifice their settlement for the technically advanced people. Bashiam represents the new generation of tribal young men who welcome technological advancement. Helen observes the tribesmen as simple, accommodating, docile, submissive and tolerant. Usually uneducated and unskilled as they are, they work as servants, cooks and labourers. But Bashiam is an exception. Being a skilled technician he comes to the fold of the English engineers and becomes a mediator between the civilized and the primitive. Like Arun Joshi, Kamala Markandaya also points to the inhuman attitude of the civilized people towards the tribes who are reduced to machine. Like Billy Biswas, Helen protests against the white man's indifferent and antagonistic attitude towards the natives. She considers Clinton responsible for Bashiam's injury. Fed up with her husband's authoritarian conduct, she drives herself into Bashiam's arms. Clinton consoles himself thinking that, 'The country's affecting her, its getting on her nerves : Well, she's not the first person it's happened to nor by any means the last' (105). Helen with her boundless curiosity about the country is an antithesis of Clinton, for whom concrete and steel are more important than human beings.

II

The predominant concern of Anita Desai as a novelist is not with the sociological, but with the psychological issues. She tries to explore the disturbed psyche of the protagonists, the interior landscape of the mind. She tells the harrowing tale of blunted human relationships. Kamala Markandaya's characters are troubled with their problems of physical survival. Nathan, Rukmani, Ravi and Nalini are busy fighting against the annihilating forces of hunger and starvation. Mira and Richard descending from affluent section of society fail to sustain their closeness due to political causes. Srinivas meets his tragic end on racial grounds. Dandekar and Sarojini in a typical middle-class set up are implicated in domestic problems arising from environmental pressures. But in Anita Desai's world the crucial issues come from within.

Desai's early novels *Cry the Peacock* (1963), *Voices in the City* (1965) and *Bye Bye Blackbird* (1971) are concerned with the problem of incompatibility in man-woman relationship. In Kamala Markandaya's novels Nathan and Rukmani, Ravi and Nalini, Srinivas and Vasantha, Appa and Amma, Sarojini and Dandekar — all have their children to support them, to mitigate their tension and soften their misery. But Maya and Goutam, Monisha and Jiban are childless couples, who suffer the agony of loneliness, despair and frustration. In *Where Shall We Go This Summer* (1975) Sita who is married to a prosperous industrialist, Raman is disgusted with his obsession with money and she escapes into a fanciful existence in an island. In *Fire on the Mountain* (1977) an extra-marital affair creates in Nanda Kaul sickness of soul and mental unhappiness. Sashi Paul points out Anita Desai's delineation of the existential crisis in the man-woman relationship in modern society :

> Desai's protagonists are highly sensitive and terribly bewildered by the burden of living helplessly in the society with absurd realities. Therefore, her fictional world is full of imperfection and unfulfilment, hankering and helplessness, agony and anger, struggle

> and surrender. She is essentially a novelist of existential concerns (39).

Anita Desai's *The Village by the Sea* (1982) which she calls a 'long story,' is an exception. It deals with the social theme of change in the old order of an Indian rural community. Hari and Lila with their two sisters, Bela and Kamala, a sick-mother and a drunkard father, find it difficult to run the family in the small fishing village Thul. Poverty forces them to sell their boats and buffalo. A village boy Ramu encourages Hari to leave fishing and instead work in the factory to get daily wages. The slow and gradual process of industrialization brings tremendous change in the rural set up :

> Oh, that is only the watchman's hut. First they send a watchman. Then they send their materials, so he can guard them. Soon they will be sending bulldozers and earth movers and steam-rollers. They are going to widen the highway — make it twice as broad. Then their machines can be brought here. Then they will build houses for their workers. The workmen will come. The factories will be built (13).

Hari cannot accept such drastic changes taking place in village. He feels startled and asks, 'And what will happen to the hill and the temple on the top?' (13). He is accustomed to digging out stones, pulling roots, preparing a small field for a winter crop of vegetables, bringing coconut from the trees and catching fish. He feels excited as Mr. De Saliva with his family and baggage comes to the village to start and run the factory business. Like Ravi in *A Handful of Rice*, Arjun and Tambi in *Nectar in a Sieve*, Hari aspires for a job in the factory. Like Munoo, the coolie, he is drawn to the life in the city :

> He knew he could never earn enough in Thul to hold his whole family. He would have to go to Bombay. Bombay was a great city, a rich city, a city crowded with people, who had jobs, earned money and made fortunes (46).

Like Kamala Markandaya, Anita Desai shows in this story how the poor farmers and fishermen leave their traditional vocations and go to cities in search of jobs. Leaving the green paddy fields and coconut plants behind, Hari joins the millions of pavement dwellers who have immigrated from the villages to work in factories. He finds workers living in slums. Their houses are built with tin-can, rag and plastic sheet. Besides factory, there is also job opportunity with the builders and the road makers. He is fed up with the polluted atmosphere of the city, with the foul-smelling gutters, the unclean bazaars and traffic congestion. He goes back to his native land, Thul. In Thul, Hari notices signs of transformation. To his amazement, the highway has been widened, the railway bridge is under construction and above all a hospital has been set up. He is glad to see his mother cured and father turning into a responsible person. The family peace is restored with all members living happily together with better financial prospects. Thus, Hari's homeward journey is similar to Rukmani's as both realize that the return of the native brings peace, tranquility and consolation. Like Hari, Rikki, the orphan fisherman boy of Markandaya's *Pleasure City* feels enchanted with the prospects of good earning in the westernized pleasure resort. But Hari is soon disillusioned and longs to get back to his village and the traditional occupation of farming.

Both Kamala Markandaya and Anita Desai show that in spite of the feeling of superiority and imperialistic outlook, some Britishers are nevertheless sympathetic towards the poor and ignorant Indians. The English technocrats and bureaucrats try to instill in the minds of the Indians rationalistic spirit and a favourable view of technological advancement. Like Dr. Kenny and Dr. Radcliffe, De Saliva is a missionary soul who takes all care of Hari's sick mother in his newly established hospital. In Dr. Kenny's hospital, the small orphan boy, Puli, gets proper treatment for his leprosy. Inspite of racial hatred from his adversary, Srinivas, the leper gets all humanitarian sympathy and care from Dr. Radcliffe. Whenever necessity demands, these Englishmen come to rescue and uplift the dejected souls. For the ignorant but sensitive village woman Rukmani, the tanning industry disrupts the tranquil village life, but finally she accepts the new order in the changing society like Selvam and Hari. The fertilizer factory in Thul widens the scope of better earning for the local residents. Thus, in spite of strained relationship between the East and the West, both Kamala Markandaya and Anita Desai present English characters that are deeply human and compassionate.

Ruth Prawar Jhabvala's novels are a study of the life-styles of the Indian upper-class and middle-class families, mostly joint families. The characters in Jhabvala's novels are from both Indian Hindus and European expatriates. There are no religious, political or racial issues as in Kamala Markandaya's novels. The backwardness of the country is attributed to the uneducated, semi-developed, over populated and conservative middle-class families. In her first novel *To Whom She Will* (1955) the parental interruption and injunctions in the young people's affairs have been ironically sneered at. Amrita's love for Hari has been misdirected and diverted towards Krishna. Hari marries Sushila not for love, but out of social compulsion. Vasant A. Shahane comments on the self-discovery of the young people at a time of social change :

> The young men and women in *To Whom She Will* are caught up in a crucial phase of social change from a convention-ridden and tradition-bound society to an open, uninhibited society free from the shackles of social customs and conventional constraints (36).

These shifting values in Hindu society have been similarly studied in *Nectar in a Sieve*. Rukmani, as well as the rural community accepts the albino child of Ira. In spite of strong resentment against industrialization in their locality such consequences of urbanization are accepted without objection. Meena Shirwadkar in her study of the status of women in family and society justifies Ira's stand, "She flouts the moral code and disobeys her mother who looks on helplessly, but her silent sacrifice exemplifies the extent to which a girl could go to help the members of her family" (29).

Markandaya, Ananda and Bhattacharya show girls suffering from poverty, repression and family restrictions. They have no sense of identity, no self-awareness. The ideal of girlhood to obey the elders and follow the tradition has been enforced upon them. Some sensitive girls resist this imposition and suffer both physically and mentally. But in *A Silence of Desire* Dandekar who cannot tolerate women's liberation and free thought finally submits to his wife's will. Sarojini accepts his proposal for a surgical operation. She has indomitable faith which enables her to survive and to win in the battle for life. In fact, this is the only novel of Kamala Markandaya which ends with the happy note of reconciliation between husband and wife after the resolution of their spiritual conflicts.

Jhabvala's second novel *The Nature of Passion* (1956) is a comedy of social manners in an upper class family. Lalaji, a millionaire has knit his big family together with the power of his wealth. His youngest daughter Nimmi grows with the consciousness of her status in an aristocratic society. She rebels against the family code when she observes her sister Rani overloaded with jewellery and Usha marrying early without protest. But she also adjusts herself to the family tradition by rejecting the love of a Parsi boy, Pheroze. She turns towards Kuku, the family choice. Thus, with her marriage to the boy of her family's choice, Nimmi feels helpless and all her idea of independence proves an illusion. In *Two Virgins* Kamala Markandaya also shows the reactions of two girls Lalitha and Saroja as they grow up physically to the social conventions regarding education, marriage and manners of women. If Lalitha revolts against the existing code of conduct, Saroja submits to it. But while Jhabvala narates the story of liberation and rebellion of women in a comic vein, Kamala Markandaya is serious and critical. Saroja learns about the consequences of such breakdown of tradition from the tragic and bitter experience of her sister. *Two Virgins* ends with a tragic irony presented in the loss of innocence of one of the vivgins through agonising experiences. Jhabvala explores the comic and ironic currents in a situation which Markandaya sees as painful experiences.

In *Esmond in India* (1958) Jhabvala studies the lives of pretentious, cultured and sophisticated people among the Indians and the Europeans. The contrasting status of Har Dayal's affluence and Ram Nath's simplicity and modesty have been drawn vividly. Esmond marries an Indian girl Gulab, but is not satisfied with her traditionalities. Har Dayal cannot accept the proposal of his daughter Shakuntala's marriage with Ram Nath's son Narayan. Shakuntala is used to a life of luxury, with servants to attend her and ornaments to decorate her. She cannot adjust to Narayan's zeal for free medical services to the poor villagers. She enjoys her youth in the company of some fashionable Indians and English ladies and gents. In their visit to Agra she has been seduced by Esmond who has dissociated himself from his wife. Jhabvala shows educated girls from upper and middle-class families cherish romantic ideals of love and marriage, but when they step down to reality, they pass through painful experience and realize the errors they have committed.

In *Some Inner Fury*, Markandaya gives a different picture of the relations of the freedom fighter Mira and her English lover Richard. Mira sacrifices her love for the sake of the country. Here, political issues and the racial rancour cause the two lovers to drift apart. Marital happiness and national causes are mutually related goals in Mira's life, hence the impossibility of their union. She deserves sympathy like Gulab who as a neglected wife passes through horrible experiences in mixed marriage. But Shakuntala's loss of innocence gets no sympathy. As Heydn Moore Williams comments on Jhabvala's attitude, 'It is the sophisticated, the intelligent, the ambitious, the materialistic, who are fundamentally the lost and the unhappy of Jhabvala's world' (33). When Gulab finds herself unprotected and insecure because of Esmond's estrangement, she does not hesitate to leave him and stay with her parents for security. Thus, the Sita-Savitri image of a Hindu housewife has eventually undergone transformation.

In *The Householder* (1960), Jhabvala presents marital discord and domestic conflict as a typical Indian middle-class problem. Prem, the Hindu teacher in a private college for rich students fails as a teacher, as a husband and householder. The demand for increase in salary, the wife's disgust with inadequate income lead to family conflict which is usual in middle-class families. In *Get Ready for Battle* (1962) Jhabvala speaks of the tyranny of a big Punjabi businessman, Gulzari Lal. In Delhi's urban society, the rich merchant's materialistic attitude leads to his estrangement from his wife, Sarala Devi who eventually finds solace in turning to social service and helping the poor and the exploited.

In *A Backward Place* (1965) the Indian poverty and difficult living conditions of the middle-classes have been studied. In this novel, Jhabvala presents the reactions of three expatriates, Judy, Clarissa and Etta, to Indian social conditions. Judy, an English girl marries an Indian boy Bal and settles with him in a middle-class joint family in Delhi. She tries to adapt herself to the requirements of Indian culture. She gets a job of typist-*cum*-receptionist in Mrs Kaul's cultural organization. A clear contrasting picture of Indian poor and the privileged class has been drawn against Mrs. Kaul's aristocratic set up, '...it was a house accustomed to much high-class entertaining and that it has that very hushed, abnormally orderly air about it characteristic of places in which not very much ordinary living is encouraged to go on' (99-100). In contrast to this picture of elegance and luxury there is the portrait of the humble servant's abode. They have perspiring bodies under their starched uniform and like other people's servants, they live eight to a room in some insanitary quarters, drowning their agony in drink and beating their wives. Judy observes the pitiable condition of the starving beggars, sickly women and their unclad and unfed children. Etta is surprised to see Judy so much inclined towards the Indians. She has been trapped by the money power of the rich hotelier, Guppy. She dreams of concerts, theatres, elegant meals and regrets bitterly for having to live in such an uncivilized country. Finally, she decides to leave this backward country. Her friend Clarissa aptly comments on her, 'A person like Etta has no right to be here at all. She simply does not grasp that India calls for spiritual adjustment' (159). Just as Caroline, in *Possession*, is convinced of the Indian state of 'wilderness' (220) from which she picks up Val, Etta adheres to her contemptuous attitude towards Indian poverty and backwardness, Hence she cannot but retreat to her own country. In *Heat and Dust* (1975) Jhabvala presents a contrasting picture of the aristocratic splendour and the lower middle class grimness. Kamala Markandaya in her novel *The Golden Honeycomb* similarly presents the glamorous living of the stately princes and the humble living of the commoners in contrast.

III

In one sense, Kamala Markandaya's novels reflect a general pre-occupation with class-consciousness represented in almost all major modern Indian novels in English. But, of course, each novelist charts his or her own paradigm of space, time and human action to embody this consciousness. Markandaya's scheme is governed by a global view of Indian socio-economic ethos in rural, semi-urban and urban settings. The time she chooses is one of crucial transition from colonial to post-colonial order. People from the urban and rural India, from inside the country and outside, from the plain land and the hilly land, from the lower class and the upper class, all have been given justice in Markandaya's portrait gallery. Like all great writers she is aware of the nature of the world and the time in which she lives. Her fictional world is peopled by men and women of all classes whose self is wounded in the seemingly interminable process of tension and conflict between freedom and necessity, between individual and society.

Works Cited

Anand, Mulk Raj. *Coolie*. New Delhi : Arnold Heinemann, 1981.

Asnani, Shayam M. "East-West Encounter in Kamala Markandaya's Later Novels." *Triveni.* 48. No. 4 (1980).

Banerji, Niroj. *Kamala Markandaya : A Critical Study*. Allahabad : Kitab Mahal, 1990.

Bhattacharya, B. *So many Hungers*. New Delhi : Orient Paper back. 1978. *He who Rides a Tiger*. New Delhi : Hind pocket Books 1955.

Chandha, Ramesh. *Cross-Cultural interaction in Indian English Fiction* : An Analysis of the Novels of Ruth Prawar Jhabvala *and Kamala Markandaya*. New Delhi : National Book Organisation, 1988.

..."Cross Cultural interaction in Markandaya's *Pleasure City.*" *The New Indian Novel in English : A study of the* 1980s. Ed. Viney Kirpal, New Delhi : Allied Publishers Ltd., 1990.

Chandrasekharan, K.R. "East and West in the Novel of Kamala Markandaya." *Critical Essays on Indian Writing in English.* Ed. M.K. Naik, S.K. Desai and G.S. Amur, Karnataka University 1968. Calcutta : Macmillan, 1977.

Chauhan, P.S. "Kamala Markandaya : Sense and Sensibility." *Literary Criterion*. 12, No. 2 and 3 (1975).

Desai, Anita. *The Village by the Sea*. Middle Sex, England : Penguin Book, 1982.

Drum, Alice. "Kamala Markandaya's Modern Quest Tale." *World Literature written in English*. 22. No. 2 (1983).

Dube, S.C. *Indian Society*. New Delhi : National Book Trust, (1990).

Dwivedi, A.N. and Niroj Banerji. "The Narrative Technique of Kamala Markandaya." *Essays in Criticism on Indian Literature in English.* Ed. Nagarajan, M.S. *et. al.*, New Delhi : S. Chand and Co., 1991.

Indra, C.T. "The True Voice of Endurance : A study of Rukmani in Markandaya's *Nectar in a Sieve.*" *Feminism and Recent Fiction in English.* Ed. Sushila Singh, New Delhi; Prestige, 1991.

Iyengar, K.R. Srinivasa. "The women Novelists." *Indian Writing in English.* New Delhi : Sterling Publisher, 1990.

Jha, Rama. "Kamala Markandaya : An overview." *Perspectives on Indian Fiction in English.* Ed. M.K. Naik, New Delhi : Abhinav Publisher, 1985.

Jha, Rekha. "*The Novels of Kamala Markandaya and Ruth Jhabvala : A Study in East-West Encountger.* New Delhi : Prestige Books, 1990.

Jhabvala, R.P. *A Backward Place.* New Delhi : Orient paperback, Hind Pocket Book, 1965.

Joseph, Margaret P. *Kamala Markandaya.* New Delhi : Arnold Heinemann, 1980.

Joshi, Arun. *The Foreigner.* New Delhi : Hind Pocket Book, 1968. *The Strange Case of Bilₗy Biswas.* New Delhi : Hind Pocket Book, 1971.

Juneja, P. "The East-West Theme : *Some Inner Fury, The Serpent and the Rope and A Dream in Hawaii.*" *Commonwealth Fiction.* Ed. R.K. Dhawan, I. New Delhi : L. Classical Publisher's 1988.

Katamble, V.D. "Kamala Markandaya's *The Coffer Dams*" An Apology for Techno-Industrialisation of Rural India." *Littcrit* II, No. 1, 2 (1985).

Krishnaswamy, Shanta. "Kamala Markandaya : Autonomy, Nurturance and the sisterhood of Man." *Glimpses of woman in India.* New Delhi : Ashish Publishing House, 1983.

Kuppuswamy, B. *Social Change in India.* New Delhi : Konark Publishers, 1993.

Mahajan, A. "*Tradition and Modernity in Markandaya's A Silence of Desire.*" *Indian Scholar.* 5, No.1 and 2 (Jan., July, 1983).

Markandaya Kamala. *Nectar in a Sieve*. New York : Signet Classic, 1954.

....*Some Inner Fury*. London : Putnam and Co., 1955.

....*A Silence of Desire* : London : Putnam and Co., 1960.

....*Possession*. London : Putnam and Co., 1963.

....*A Handful of Rice*. New Delhi : Orient Paper-backs, 1985.

....*The Coffer Dams*. New-Delhi : Orient Paper-backs, 1969.

....*The Nowhere Man*. Bombay : Orient Longman, Ltd. Ed. Sangam, 1975.

....*Two Virgins*. New Delhi : Vikas Publishing House, Ed. Bell Book, 1977.

....*The Golden Honeycomb*. London : Chatto and Windus, 1977.

....*Pleasure City*. London : Chatto and Windus, 1982.

Menon, K.M. and K.V.K. Rao. *The Coffer Dams* : "A Critical Study." *Perspectives on Kamala Markandaya*. Ed. M. Prasad, Ghaziabad : Vimal Prakashan, 1981.

Nicholson, Kai. *A Presentation of Social Problems in the Indio-Anglian and Anglo-Indian Novel*. Bombay : Jaico Publishing House, 1972.

Parameswaran, Uma. "Native Aliens and Expatriates : Kamala Markandaya and Balachandra Rajan." *A Study of Representative Indo English Novelists*. New Delhi : Vikas Publications, 1976.

Pathania, Usha. "March to Autonomy." *Human Bonds and Bondages : The Fiction of Anita Desai and Kamala Markandaya*. New Delhi : Kanishka Publishing House, 1992.

Paul Shashi. 'Alienation to Existentialism : A Study of Anita Desai's Novels.' *The Quest*, June 1995.

Pollard, Arthur. "Kamala Markandaya's *The Golden Honeycomb*." *Through Different Eyes*. Ed. Kirpal Singh, Calcutta : Writers Workshop. 1984.

Prasad, H.M. 'The Fictional Epic on Indian Life : A Study on Theme and Technique of *Nectar in a Sieve*.' *Perspectives on Kamala Markandaya*. Ed. M. Prasad, Ghaziabad : Vimal Prakashan, 1984.

Raizada, Harish. "East-West Confrontation in the Novels of Kamala Markandaya." *Perspectives on Kamala Markandaya*. Ed. Madhusudan Prasad, Ghaziabad : Vimal Prakashan, 1984.

Rama Moorthi P. 'My Life is my own. A Study of Shashi Despande's Women.' *Feminism and Recent Fiction in English*. Ed. S. Singh, New Delhi : Prestige Books, 1991.

Rao, A.K. Srinivas. 'The Novels of Kamala Markandaya. A study.' *Studies in Contemporary Indian Fiction in English*. Ed. A.N. Dwivedi. Allahabad : Kitab Mahal, 1987.

Rao, A.V. Krishna. 'Feminine Sensibility in Indo-Anglian Fiction' *Triveni*. 35, No. 4 (Jan. 1967).

....'The Novels of Kamala Markandaya : A Study.' *Studies in Contemporary Indian Fiction in English*. Ed. A.N. Dwivedi, Allahabad : Kitab Mahal, 1987.

....'Continuity and change in the Novels of Kamala Markandaya.' *Perspectives on Kamala Markandaya*. Ed. M. Prasad, Ghaziabad : Vimal Prakash, 1984.

Rao, G. Nageswara. "Betwixt Negation and Affirmation : An Approach to *A Silence of Desire*." *When East Meets West : Indian thought in Anglo-Indian and Indo-English Fiction*. Ed. A.R. Rao and M. Sivaramakrishna, New Delhi : Sterling Publishers, 1994.

Rao, K.S.N. "Lovc, Sex, Marriage, and Morality in Kamala Markandaya's Novels." *Osmania Journal of English Studies*. 10. No. 1 (1973).

...."*A Slience of Desire*." *The Indian PEN*. 35. No. 12, (Dec. 1969).

Rao, Raja *Kanthapura*. New York : New Directions, 1963.

Riemenschneider, D. "British Characters in Indo-English Fiction." *Aspects of Indian Writing in English*. Ed. M.K. Naik, New Delhi : Macmillan, 1979.

Rao, N. Susheela. "England in the Novels of Kamala Markandaya." *Journal of Indian Writing in English*. 15, No. 1, Jan. 1987.

Reddy, K.V. 'Why Don't I die : Coolie,' *Major Indian Novelists*. New Delhi : Prestige, 1990.

Sanyal, Samares C. "Thematic Preoccupations of the Indo-Anglian Novelists : An Indian Consciousness." *Indianness in Major Indo-Anglian Novels*. Bareilly : Prakash Book Depot, 1984.

Shahane, V.A. *Ruth Prawer Jhabvala*. New Delhi : Arnold Heneimann, 1976.

Shirwadker, K. *Image of Woman in the Indo-Anglian Novel*. New Delhi : Sterling Publishers, 1979.

Singh R.S. "West Meets East : A study of Kamala Markandaya's *Possession.*" *Image of India in the Indian Novel in English, 1960-1985*. Ed. S. Pandey and R. Raja Rao. Bombay : Orient Longman, 1993.

Srivastava, R.K. "Sdymbolic Triumvirate in *A Handful of Rice*." *Six Indian Novelists in English*. Amritsar : Guru Nanak Dev. University Press, 1987.

Thumboo Edwin. "Kamala Markandaya's *A Silence of Desire*." *Through Different Eyes*. Ed. Kirpal Singh. Calcutta : Writers Workshop, 1984.

Varma, R.M. "The Bi-cultural world of Kamala Markandaya's Novels." *Some Aspects of Indo-English Fiction*. New Delhi : Jainsons Publications, 1985.

Williams, H.M. *The Fiction of Ruth Prawer Jhabvala*. Calcutta : Writers Workshop, 1973.

Select Bibliography

(I) Kamala Markandaya's Works

A. Fiction

Nectar in a Sieve. London : Putnam, 1954.

Some Inner Fury. London : *Putnam and Co.* 1955.

A Silence of Desire. London : Putnam and Co. 1960.

Possession. London : Putnam and Co. 1963.

A Handful of Rice. London : Hamish Hamilton, 1966.

The Coffer Dams. London : Hamish Hamilton, 1969.

The Nowhere Man. New York : The John Day Co. 1972.

Two Virgins. New York : The John Day Co. 1973.

The Golden Honeycomb. London : Chatto and Windus, 1977.

Pleasure City. London : Chatto and Windus, 1982.

'The Plan' a short story. *The Illustrated Weekly of India.* 24 Aug. 1965, 9-11.

'Return Ticket', a short story. *The Illustrated Weekly of India.* 14 Aug. 1966, 21-23.

B. Non-Fiction

'Why do we write in English' *Adam.* 5, *International Review* (1971), 355-360.

'On images' paper presented during the seminar on socio literature at the East-West centre for cultural Interchange in Honolulu, Aug. 1973. 'Reminiscences of Rural India,' *John Kenneth Galbraith Introduces India.* Ed. John Kenneth Galbraith. New Delhi : Vikash Publishing House, 1974.

'One pair of Eyes, some Random Reflections,' addressed to the European Branch of ACLALS, which met in Stirling Scotland, April 1975, *The Literary Criterion* 11, 4 (1975).

C. Interviews

'A Novelist of India Reflects Two Worlds' (Interview). *The New York*, Tuesday, (17 July, 1973).

Interview of Susheela N. Rao with Kamala Markandaya on May 1977, at Cambridge, England, discussion on *The Golden Honeycomb*.

Letter to Margaret P. Joseph on 9 Oct. 1976 carrying the authors condemnation of racial prejudice and cruelty to any living being.

(II) Works on Kamala Markandaya

A. Books

Aithal, S.K. and Rashmi Aithal. "Indo English Fictional Experiments with Inter-racial and Inter cultural Relationships." *Alien Voice : Perspectives on Commonwealth Literature*. Ed. A.K. Srivastava. Lucknow : Print House, 1981.

Asnani, Sham, M. 'Quest for Identity theme in three Commonwealth Novels : *Alien Voice : Perspectives on Common-wealth Literature*. Ed. A.K, Srivastava. Lucknow : Print House, 1981.

Asnani, S.M. and Deepika Rajpal. "Identity crisis in *The Nowhere Man* and *Wife*." *Quest for Identity in Indian English Writing*. I. Fiction. Ed. R.S. Pathak. New Delhi : Bahri Publications, 1992.

Badal, R.K., *Kamala Markandaya*. Bareilly : Prakash Depot. 1973.

Bande, Usha. "Raj : A Thematic Study." *Indian Women Novelists*. Ed. R.K. Dhawan. New Delhi : Prestige, Vol. 5, 1992.

Banerji, Niroj. *Kamala Markandaya : A Thematic Study*. New Delhi : Sarup and Sons, 1995.

Chadha, Ramesh. *Cross-Cultural Interaction in Indian English Fiction : An Analysis of the Novels of Ruth Prawar Jhabvala and Kamala Markandaya*. New Delhi : National Book Organisation, 1988.

.... "Cross Cultural Interaction in Markandaya's *Pleasure City*." *The New Indian Novel in English : A Study of the 1980s*. Ed. Viney Kirpal. New Delhi : Allied Publishers, Ltd. 1990.

Chandra, Subhas. "City in the Novels of Kamala Markandaya, Anita Desai and Shashi Despande." *Indian Women Novelists*. Ed. R.K. Dhawan, New Delhi : Prestige, Vol. I, 1992.

Chandrasekharan K.R. "East and West in the Novels of Kamala Markandaya." *Critical Essays on Indian Writing in English*. Ed. M.K. Naik, S.K. Desai and G.S. Amur, Karnataka University : 1968, Calcutta : Macmillan, 1977.

Chatterjee, Arundhati. "Rukmani, The Mother Figure in *Nectar in a Sieve*." *Studies in Indian Fiction in English* Ed. G.S.B. Gupta, Gulberga : *Journal of Indian writing in English*, Publication, 1987.

Class Consciousness in the novels of Kamala Markandaya by Dr. Pravati Misra Reader in English, S.B. Women's College, Cuttak, Orissa.

Dale, James. "Kamala Markandaya and the outsider." *Individual and Community in Commonwealth Literature*. Ed. Deniel Massa, Malta : University of Malta, 1979.

Dwivedi, A.N. "*The Golden Honeycomb* : A Critical Appraisal." *Papers on Indian Writing in English*, part-II. New Delhi : Amar Prakashan, 1991.

"The Narrative Technique of Kamala Markandaya." *Essays in Criticism on Indian Literature in English*. Ed. Nagarajan M.S. *et. al.* New Delhi : S. Chand and Co., 1991.

"Indian Fiction in English : Retrospect and prospect." *Studies in Contemporary Indian Fiction in English*. Allahabad : Kitab Mahal, 1989.

Garg, P. "The March of the Tricolour." *The Freedom Movement in Indian Fiction in English*. New Delhi : Asha Publishing House, 1993.

Ghorpade, Pradnya Viyaj. Rural India as Reflected in Kamala Markandaya's *Nectar in a Sieve*. *Studies in Indian writing in English*, Vol. I. Ed. R. Mittapalli and P.P. Piciucco. New Delhi : Atlantic Publishers and Distributors, 2000.

Guru Prasad, T. "And Never the Twain shall Meet : Kamala Markandaya's *The Nowhere Man*." *Explorations in Modern*

Indo-English Fiction. Ed. R.K. Dhawan. New Delhi : Bahri Publications, 1992.

Harrex, S.C. "A sense of Identity : The Early Novels of Kamala Markandaya." *The Fire and the Offering* Vol-I. Ed. P. Lal, Calcutta : Writers Workshop, 1977.

Hemenway, S. "Kamala Markandaya." *The Indo-Anglian Novel, The Novel of India*, Vol-II. Calcutta : Writers Workshop, 1975.

Inamdar, F.A. "Image and symbol Pattern in Kamala Markandaya's Novels." *Indian Writing in English,* Vol-I. Ed. M.K. Bhatnagar, New Delhi : Atlantic Publishers and Distributors, 1996.

Indra, C.T. "The True Voice of Endurance : A study of Rukmani in Markandaya's *Nectar in a Sieve*." *Feminism and Recent Fiction in English,* Ed. Sushila Singh. New Delhi : Prestige, 1991.

Iyengar, K.R.S. "The Women Novelists." *Indian Writing in English*. New Delhi : Sterling Publisher, 1990.

Jha, Rama. "Kamala Markandaya : An overview." *Perspectives on Indian Fiction in English*. Ed. M.K. Naik. New Delhi : Abhinav Publishers, 1985.

Jha, Rekha. *The Novels of Kamala Markandaya and Ruth Jhabvala : A Study in East-West Encounter*. New Delhi : Prestige Books, 1990.

Jain, N.K. "Kamala Markandaya : *Nectar in a Sieve*." *Major Indian Novels : An Evaluation*. Ed. N.S. Pradhan. New Delhi : Arnold Heinemann, 1985.

Jeyaraju, M.A. and D. Miruthula. 'Kamala Markandaya's *The Golden Honeycomb* as a post colonical novel.' Critical studies on Indian Fiction in English. Ed. R.A. Singh and V.N. Kumar. New Delhi : Atlantic Publishers, 1999.

Joseph, Margaret P. *Kamala Markandaya*. New Delhi : Arnold Heinemann, 1980.

Juneja, P. "The East-West Theme : *Some Inner Fury, The Serpent and the Rope and A Dream in Hawii*." *Commonwealth*

Fiction. Ed. R.K. Dhawan, Vol-I. New Delhi : Classical Publishers, 1988.

Kalinnikova, E.J. "The Hindus Woman from London : Kamala Markandaya." *Indian English Literature : a Perspective*. Ghaziabad : Vimala Prakashan, 1982.

Khan, F.A. "Kamala Markandaya." *Cultural Imperialism and the Indo-English Novel-Myth Vs. Realism, East Vs. West*. pennsylvania : The Pennsylvania State University Press, 1993.

Kirpal, Viney. *The Third World Novel of Expatriation : A Study of Emigre Fiction by Indian, West African and Caribbean Writers*. New Delhi : Sterling Publishers, 1989.

Krishnaswamy, S. "Kamala Markandaya : Autonomy, Nurturance and the sisterhood of Man, *"Glimpses of woman in India."* New Delhi : Ashish Publishing House, 1985.

Marathe, Sunita and Viney Kirpal. "The Immigrant Experience : A comparison of Anita Desai's *Bye Bye Blackbird and Markandaya's The Nowhere Man." Indian Women Novelists*, Vol-I. Ed. R.K. Dhawan. New Delhi : Prestige, 1993.

Maya, D. *Narrating Colonialism : Post Colonial Images of the British in Indian English Fiction*. New Delhi : Prestige Books, 1997.

Mehta, M.L. "The Exploited Peasant in Indo-English Novel." *Contemporary Indian English Fiction : An Anthology of Essays*. Ed. K.N. Awasthi. Jalandhar : ABS Publications, 1993.

Mehta P.P. *Indo-Anglian Fiction : An Assessment*. Bareilly : Prakash Book Depot, 1968.

Meerabai, K. "Method and Narrative Technique in Kamala Markandaya's *Nectar in a Sieve, Anita Desai's Cry, The Peacock,* Nayantara Sahgal's *A Time to be Happy* and Ruth Jhobvala's *Heat and Dust*." *Indian Women Novelists*. Vol-I. Ed. R.K. Dhawan. New Delhi : Prestige, 1991.

Mittapali, Rajendar. "Myth as Macro Structure : A Reading of Kamala Markandaya's *A Silence of Desire* and Nayantara Sahgal's The Day in Shadow. *Studies in Indian writing in English*. Vol-I. Ed. R. Mittapalli and P.P. Piciucco. New Delhi. Atlantic Publishers and Distributors, 2000.

Mukherjee Meenakshi. *The Twice Born Fiction : Themes and Techniques of the Indian Novel in English.* New Delhi : Heinemann, 1971.

Mukherjee Sujit. "The Indian Novelist in English as Best Seller." *Indian Literature of the Past Fifty Years* (1917-1967). Ed. C.D. Narasimhaiah. Mysore : University of Mysore. 1970.

Naik M.K. "The Achievement of Indian English Fiction." *Dimensions of Indian English Literature.* New Delhi : Sterling Publishers, 1983.

... "Kamala Markandaya." *A History of Indian English Literature,* r.p.t. New Delhi : Sahitya Academy, 1989.

Nicholson, Kai. *A presentation of social problems in the Indo-Anglian and Anglo-Indian Novel.* Bombay : Jaico Publishing House, 1972.

Parameswaran, Uma. "Native Aliens and Expatriates : Kamala Markandaya and Balachandra Rajan." *A Study of Representative Indo-English Novelists.* New Delhi : Vikas Publications, 1976.

... *Kamala Markandaya : Writers of the Indian Diaspora.* New Delhi : Rawat Publishers, 2000.

Pollard, Arthur. "Kamala Markandaya's *The Golden Honeycomb" Through Different Eyes.* Ed. Kirpal Singh. Calcutta : Writers Workshop, 1984.

Prasad, H.M. "Theme of Exile in Indo-English Novels." *Perspectives on Commonwealth Literature.* Ed. A.K. Srivastava. Lucknow : Print House, 1981.

... "The Quintessence of Kamala Markandaya's Art." *Response : Recent Revelations of Indian Fiction in English.* Bareilly : Prakash Book Depot. 1983.

Prasad, V.V.N. Rajendra. "The Indian Novel in English : Its Socio-Cultural Milieu." *The Self, the Family and Society in Five Indian Novelists.* New Delhi : Prestige, 1990.

Pathania, Usha. "March to Autonomy, "Human Bonds and Bondages : *The Fiction of Anita Desai and Kamala Markandaya.* New Delhi : Kanishka Publishing House, 1992.

Rao, A.V. Krishna. *The Indo-Anglian Novel and the changing Tradition : A Study of the Novels of Mulk Raj Anand, Kamala Markandaya, R.K. Narayan and Raja Rao,* 1930-1964. Mysore : Rao and Raghavan, 1972.

... "Golden Honeycomb : A Brief Study," *Studies in Indian Fiction in English.* Ed. G.S.B. Gupta. Gulberga : Journal of Indian Writing in English Publication, 1987.

... "The Novels of Kamala Markandaya : A study." *Studies in Contemporary Indian Fiction in English.* Ed. A.N. Dwivedi. Allahabad : Kitab Mahal, 1987.

Rao, G. Nageswara. "Betwixt Negation and Affirmation : An Approach to *A Silence of Desire.*" *When East meets West : Indian thought in Anglo-Indian and Indo-English Fiction.* Ed. A.R. Rao and M. Sivaramakrishna. New Delhi : Sterling Publishers, 1994.

Raizada, Harish. "East-West Confrontation in the Novels of Kamala Markandaya." *Perspectives on Kamala Markandaya.* Ed. Madhusudan Prasad. Ghaziabad : Vimal Prakashan, 1984.

Ramamurti, K.S. "*Two Virgins* : A problem Novel." *Search for Identity : Modern Literatures and Creative Arts.* Ed. A.R. Davis. Sydney : Angus and Robertson, 1974.

Rao, Vimala C. "The Achievement of the Indian Women Novelists." *Indian Literature of the past Fifty Years* (1917-1967). Ed. C.D. Narasimhaiah. Mysore : University of Mysore, 1970.

Reddy, K.V. "A classic of the Hunger theme : *Nectar in a Sieve.*" And "A tryst with conscience : *A Handful of Rice.*" *Major Indian Novelists.* New Delhi : Prestige Books, 1990.

Riemenschneider, D. "British Characters in Indo-English Fiction." *Aspects of Indian Writing in English.* Ed. M.K. Naik. New Delhi : Macmillan, 1979.

Sanyal, Samares. C. "Thematic Preoccupations of the Indo-Anglian Novelists : An Indian Consciousness." *Indiannes in Major Indo-Anglian Novels.* Bareilly : Prakash Book Depot, 1984.

Sastry, Krishna L.S.R. "East-West Encounter in Indo-Anglian Fiction." *Essays in Studies*. Ed. G.V.L.N. Sarma. Machilipatam : Triveni Publishers, 1977.

Saxena, O.P. "The Alienated Protagonist in the Indo-English Novel." *Glimpses of Indo-English Fiction,* Vol-I. New Delhi : Jainson Publishers, 1985.

Sengupta, C. "Alienation in Kamala Markandaya's *Some Inner Fury : A Study of Characters." Indian Fiction in English : Problems and Promises*. Ed. R.S. Pathak. New Delhi : Northern Book Centre, 1990.

Shirwadker, M. *Image of woman in the Indo-Anglian Novel.* New Delhi : Sterling Publishers, 1979.

Singh, A.K. "The Element of protect in Kamala Markandaya." *Contemporary Indian Fiction in English.* Ed. A.K. Singh. New Delhi : Creative Books, 1993.

Singh, R.S. "Soulful East and Ratiocinative West, Kamala Markandaya's Novels." *Indian Novel in English. Kurukhetra* : Arnold-Heinemann, 1977.

... "West Meets East : A study of Kamala Markandaya's *Possession." Image of India in the Indian Novel in English,* 1960-1985. Ed. S. Pandey and R. Raja Rao. Bombay : Orient Longman, 1993.

Singla, Shakuntala. "Some Aspects of Inter Cultural and Inter-racial interaction in the Novels of Kamala Markandaya and R.P. Jhabvala." *Indian writings in English*, Vol. II. Ed. M.K. Bhatnagar. New Delhi : Atlantic Publishers, 1996.

Spenser, Dorothy M. *Indian Fiction in English : An Annotated Bibliography*. Philadelphia : University of Pensylvania Press, 1960.

Srivastava, R.K. *Six Indian Novelists in English.* Amritsar : Guru Nanak Dev University Press, 1987.

... "The Theme of Hunger in Bhattacharya and Markandaya." *Explorations in Modern Indo-English Fiction,* Vol-VII. Ed. R.K. Dhawan. New Delhi : Bahri Publishers, 1992.

... "Level of Colonial Consciousness in Markandaya's *Possession." Colonial Consciousness in Black American, African and*

Indian Fiction in English. Ed. R.K. Srivastava. Jalandhar : ABC, 1991.

... "Women as possessor : A Reflection of Markandaya's Anti-Patriarchal Rage and Divided — Consciousness in *Possession*." *Feminism and Recent Fiction in English*. Ed. Sushila Singh. New Delhi : Prestige, 1991.

Surendran, K.V. " 'Nectar in a Sieve' : A Tale of the Hapless and Desperate." New Perspectives on Indian and Western Fiction. New Delhi : Sarup and Sons, 2000.

Thumboo Edwin. "Kamala Markandaya's *A Silence of Desire*." *Through Different Eyes*. Ed. Kirpal Sing. Calcutta : Writers Workshop, 1984.

The Authors and Writers Who's who. "Kamala Markandaya." 5th edition, 1963, p. 326.

Varma, R.M. "The Bi-Cultural World of Kamala Markandaya's Novels," *Some Aspects of Indo-English Fiction*. New Delhi : Jainsons Publications, 1985.

Vinson, James. Ed. "Kamala Markandaya," *Contemporary Novelists*. New York : St. Martins Press, 1976.

Wakeman, John. Ed. "Kamala Markandaya," *World Authors*. New York : The H.W. Wilson Co. 1975.

Williams, H.M. "Victims and Virgins : some characters in Markandaya's Novels," *Galaxy of Indian Writers in English*. New Delhi : Akshat Publications, 1987.

... *Studies in Modern Indian Fiction in English*, Vol-II. Calcutta : Writers Workshop, 1973.

B. Journals

Adams, Phoebe. Rev. of *Nectar in a Sieve*. *Atlantic Review*. 211 (June 1963), 108.

Adkins, John F. "Kamala Markandaya : Indo-Anglian Conflict as Unity." *Journal of South Asian Literature*. 10 No. 1 (1974), 89-102.

Anjaneyulu, D. "Indian writing in English form K.S. Venkataramni to Kamala Markandaya." *Triveni*. 32 (April 1963), 19-28.

Appasamy, S.P. "*The Goldenhoneycomb* : A saga of Princely life in India by Kamala Markandaya," Journal of Indian Writing in English. 6, No. 2 (July 1978) 56-63.

Argyle, Barry. "Kamala Markandaya's *Nectar in a Sieve.*" *Ariel.* 4, No. 1 (1973) 34-45.

Asnani, Shyam M. "Character and Technique in Kamala Markandaya's Novels." *Rajasthan University Studies in English.* II (1978), 68.

... "East-West Encounter in Kamala Markanday's Later Novels." *Triveni.* 48, No. 4 (1980), 56-63.

... "Contribution of women in the Indo-English Novel." *Triveni.* 44 (Jan-Sept., 1975), 45-52.

... "The theme of Famine and Hunger : Bhabani Bhattacharya and Kamala Markandaya." *World Literature Written in English.* IXX (Spring 1980), 91-110.

Belliappa, N. Meena. "East-West Encounter : Indian Women writers of Fiction; in English." *Literary Criterion.* 8, No. 3 (1966), 18-27.

Bande, Usha. "I search, I find : Valmiki's quest in Kamala Markandaya's *Possession.*" *Osmania Journal of English Studies.* 25 (1989), 73-81.

Bharatha Lakshmi, M.V. and S. Krishna Sarma. "The Brown British : A Study of Recent Immigrant Novels," *Literary Half-Yearly.* 18, No. 2 (1976), 53-70.

Barbato, L.R. "The Arrow in the circle : Time and Reconciliation of cultures in Kamala Markandaya's *Nectar in a Sieve.*" Ariel 22, No. 4 (Oct. 1991), 7-15.

Begum, Jamela. "Glimpses of Indian Women in Kamala Markandaya's Novels." *Commonwealth Quarterly.* 13, No. 36 (March 1988).

Chadha, Mrs. Ramesh. "*Heat and Dust and The Coffer Dams* : A comparative study," *The Journal of Indian Writing in English.* 10, No. 182 (Jan.-July 1982).

Chauhan, P.S. "Kamala Markandaya : Sense and Sensibility," *Literary Criterion.* 12, No. 2 and 3 (1975), 134-47.

Desai, Anita. "Women Writers." *Quest* (April June, 1970), 39-43.

Drum, Alice. "Kamala Markandaya's Modern Quest Tale," *World Literature written in English.* 22, No. 2 (1983).

Dunn, T.A. "Intensity and crispness" *Journal of Commonwealth literature.* No. 5 (July 1968), 127.

Ezekiel, Nissim. Rev. of *Possession. Imprint.* (Feb. 1964), 188-193.

... "Puppet show" *The Illustrated Weekly of India,* (June 15, 1975), 32.

... Rev. of *Two Virgins, The Illustrated Weekly of India* (15 June 1979).

Fletcher, John. *"The Virgins," The International Fiction Review.* (Jan. 1975).

Fracht, S. "A study of Kamala Markandaya's *A Handful of Rice.*" *English Journal* 57 (Nov. 1968), 1143-1146.

Fuchs, Marcia, G. Rev. of *Pleasure city* under the title *Shalimar. Library Journal* (July 1983). 1383.

Geetha, P. "Kamala Markandaya : An Interpretation." *Commonwealth Quarterly.* 3, No. 9 (1978), 96-109.

... Images and Archetypes in Kamala Markandaya's Novels : A study in cultural Ambivalence." *The Journal of Commonwealth Literature.* No. 1 (1991), 169-178.

Gondal, Y.C. "Relationship of Dams" *Journal of Commonwealth Literature.* 3 No. 1 (June 1973).

Gooneratne, Yasmine. "Traditional Elements in the fiction of Kamala Markandaya, R.K. Narayan and Ruth Prawer Jhabvala." *World Literature Written in English.* 15, No. 1 (1975), 121-134.

Gowri, G. "Kamala Markandaya's Male Protagonists." *The Literary Half-Yearly.* 33, No. 2 (July 1992) 56-61.

Harrex, S.C. "A sense of Identity : The Novels of Kamala Markandaya." *Journal of Commonwealth Literature.* 6, No. 1 (1971) 65-78.

Hess Linda. *The Coffer Dams, Saturday Review* (14 June 1969), 35.

Hopkinson, L. Shirley. Rev. of *The Coffer Dams, Library Journal.* (15 June 1969), 2488.

Horst, M.H. "Kamala Markandaya." *New Circle.* 18, No. 7 (March 1973), 41

Indira, S. "The Nowhere man : A Comparative study of Anita Desai's *Baumgatner's Bombay,* and Kamala Markandaya's *Nowhere Man.*" *The Indian Journal of English Studies.* 30 (1991-92), 5-12.

Iredale, Roger. Society and Self-knowledge in the Novels of Kamala Markandaya." *Tenor.* No. 2 (Jan. 1979).

Jain, Jasbir. "The Novels of Kamala Markandaya," *Indian Literature.* 18, No. 2 (1975), 36-43.

Katamble, V.D. "Kamala Markandaya's *The Coffer Dams* : An Apology for Techno-Industrialisation of Rural India." Littcrit II. No. 1, 2 (1985).

Krishnamurti, M.G. "Indian fiction in English," *Humanist Review.* 1.4 (1969), 435-51.

Krupkar, B. "Race Relations and *The Nowhere man.*" *The Literary Endeavour.* 2, No. 2, 3, p. 21.

Kumar, P. Conflict and Resolutions in the Novels of Kamala Markandaya," *World Literature To-Day.* 60 (Winter 1986).

Kumar, Shiv K. "Tradition and change in the Novels of Kamala Markandaya," *Osmania Journal of English Studies.* 7, No. 1 (1969), 1-9.

Larson, Charles, R. "The Prince and the Paupers," *Book World. The Washington Post* (Feb. 6, 1977), F. 10.

... "Honored Novel." The New Republic (June 1, 1974), 30-31.

Mahajan, A. "Tradition and Modernity in Markandaya's A Silence of Desire." Indian Scholar. 5, No. 1 and 2 (Jan., July 1983), 137-144.

Mann, Charles W, Jr. Rev. of *A Handful of Rice. Library Journal.* 91 (Sep. 15, 1966), 4137.

Menon, Madhvi. Rev. of *Pleasure City*. *The Journal of Indian Writing in English.* 2 No. 2 (July 1983), 57-59.

Mohan, R. "The Rapunzel Syndrome in Indo-English fiction." *The Indian Journal of English Studies.* 31 (1992-93).

McCutchion, David. The Indian Novel in English, *"The Jadhavpur Journal of Comparative Literature.* II (1973), 1-20.

Motion, Andrew. "The Oceanic Felling : A Review of *Pleasure city*." *Time's Literary Supplement* (17, Sept. 1982), 993.

Montgomery, Ruth. "WLB Biography : Kamala Markandayam," *Wilson Library Bulletin* (Nov. 1963), 296.

Mukherjee, M. "Literature of Exile." *ACLALS Bulletin.* 4 (1974), 27-32.

... "The theme of Displacement in Anita Desai and Kamala Markandaya" *World Literature Written in English.* 17 (1978), 225-33.

Mukherjee, Sujit. "Aspects of Indo-Anglian Novel." *Quest.* (April-June 1970), 34-43.

Nambiar, K.C. Rev. of *The Coffer Dams. Osmania Journal of English Studies.* 7, No. 1 (1969).

Nanda Kumar Prema. "The Achievement of the Indo-Anglian Novelist." *Literacy Criterion.* 5, No. 1 (Winter, 1961), 152-65.

Natarajan, N. "*Heat and Dust and The Coffer Dams* : A Comparative Study." *Journal of Indian Writing in English.* 10 No. 2 (1982).

Parameswaran, Uma. "India for the western Reader : A study of Kamala Markandaya's Novels." *Texas Quarterly.* 10, No. 2 (Sum, 1968).

... "Kamala Markandaya's *Pleasure City" The CRNLE Review Journal.* No. 1 (1983), 82.

Parton, Margaret. "*A Handful of Rice*" *Saturday Review.* (Aug. 27, 1966).

Payne, Robert. "The Homesick Shepherd" *Saturday Review.* May 25 (1963), 34.

Pineral, Paul. "*Possession*" *Atalantic Review.* 226 (June 1963), 136.

Pollard, Arthur. "Kamala Markanday's *The Golden Honeycomb" The Journal of Indian Writing in English.* 8, No. 1, 2 (Jan.-July 1980), 22-26.

Prasad, H.M. "The Quintessence of Kamala Markanday's Art." *Commonwealth Quarterly.* 3. No, 9 (1978), 173-85.

Radha. K. "The Hunger and Anger of Ravi in Kamala Markanday's *A Handful of Rice.*" *The Indian Journal of English Studies.* 30 (1991-92), 13-20.

Ramamurti, K.S. "The Indian Women Novelist Writing in English." Littcrit (1980), 33-42.

... "*Two Virgins* : A problem Novel." Litterit. 7, No. 2 (Dec. 1981), 36-45.

Ram Chandran, Ragini. "*The Nowhere Man*" *Literary Criterion.* 11, No. 2, (1974).

Rao, A. V. Krishna. "Love and Hate in Markandaya's *Some Inner Fury* and Atkinson's *Pink and the Brown.*" "*Commonwealth Quarterly*" (1983-84).

Rao, Susheela N. "England in the Novels of Kamala Markandaya." *The Journal of Indian Writing in English.* 15, No. 1 (Jan. 1987).

... "Western Women in Eastern Novels : The Fiction of Kamala Markandaya." *The Literary Half-yearly.* 34, No. 1 (Jan. 1993), 51-63.

... "Kamala Markandaya : A Bibliography." *World Literature Written in English.* 20, No. 2 (1981).

Rao, Shyamala B. "Women writers in Indo-Anglian Fiction." *Century* (26-Jan. 1972).

Rao, K.S.N. "Religious Elements in Kamala Markandaya's Novels." *Ariel.* 8, No. 1 (Jan. 1977), 35-50.

... "Some Notes on the Plots of Kamala Markandaya's Novels." *Indian Literature.* 13, No. 1 (1970).

... "Love, Sex, Marriage, and Morality in Kamala Markandaya's Novels." *Osmania Journal of English Studies.* 10, No. 1 (1973), 69-79.

... "*A Silence of Desire.*" *The Indian PEN.* 35, No. 12 (Dec. 1969).

... "Kamala Markandaya. *Nectar in a Sieve.* A Footnote to the title." *The Indian PEN.* 35 (Nov. 1969).

... Kamala Markandaya's "*Possession* — The title as a key to the theme." *The Indian PEN.* (Jan. 1970), 1-3.

... Markandaya's "*Possession* and the Idea of the Triumph of the Spirit : II." *The Indian PEN* (Nov. 1970), 313-17.

... "The Novels of Kamala Markandaya : A contemporary Indo-Anglian Novelist." Literature East and West. 15, No. 2 (June 1971), 209-18.

Rao Vimala. "Kamala Markandaya." *The Literary Criterion.* (Winter, 1958).

... "Indian Expatriates." *Journal of Commonwealth Literature.* 10, No. 3 (April 1976).

Rubenstein, Roberta. "Kamala Markandaya's *Two Virgins*" *World Literature Written in English.* 13 (1973), 225-30.

Sarma, S. Krishna. "Two Recent Novels of Kamala Markandaya." *Triveni.* 45, No. 3 (1976), 28-35.

Scott, Paul. "Rev. of *A Silence of Desire, New Statesman* (26 Nov. 1960), 851.

Seebohm, Caroline. "Class and caste in India." *New York Times Book Review* (1977), 42.

Sengupta, C. "Jaxtaposition of oppositions : A study of characters in *Some Inner Fury.*" *Indian Scholar.* 11, No. 1 (Jan. 1989).

Shepherd, Ron. "Suffering in Indo-English Fiction." *Explorations in Modern Indo-English Fiction.* Ed. R.K. Dhawan. New Delhi : Bahri Publishers, 1992.

Shimer, Dorothy Blair. "Sociological Imagery in the Novels of Kamala Markandaya." *World Literature Written in English.* 14 (1975), 357-70.

Singh, R.S. "The Vision of Kamala Markandaya." *Vidya.* 9 (Jan. 1966), 45-55.

Spaulding, Martha. "The Golden Honeycomb." *The Atlantic Monthly.* Boston (1977).

Srivastava, Ramesh K. "Symbolism in *Nectar in a Sieve." Indian Scholar.* 1, No. 2 (July 1979), 115.

... "The Pattern of Hope and Fear in Markandaya's *Nectar in a Sieve." The Indian Journal of English Studies.* 20, No. 1 (1980).

... "Stability and changing social scene in Markandaya's *A Silence of Desire." The Quest.* 6, No. 2 (Dec. 1992), 1-17.

... "The Problem of Identity in Markandaya's *The Nowhere Man. The Critical Endeavour.* 3 (Oct. 1977).

... "Machines and Men in Markandaya's *The Coffer Dams. Indian Scholar.* 14, No. 2 (July 1992).

... "Limitations in *Nectar in a Sieve." Bharat Prativa.* 13, No. 1 (Spring 1989), 27-34.

... "Raging Inferno and Fumbling Inarticulacy : Limits of Narrative Technique in Kamala Markandaya's *Some Inner Furry." The Indian Journal of English Studies.* 30, New Delhi : (1991-92), 21-37.

... Srivastava, N. "Some Indian Women Writers in English." *Indian Literature.* 18, No. 4 (1975), 63-72.

... Stokes, Eric. "Generally Ravishing." *The Times Literary Supplement* (April 29, 1977), 7.

Thumboo, E. "Kamala Markandaya's *A Silence of Desire." The Journal of Indian Writing in English.* 8, No. 1 and 2 (Jan.-July 1980), 134.

Trikka, M. "*The Nowhere Man." The Indian Literary Review.* 1, No. 1 (May 1978).

Tyrner, A.G. "Indo-Anglian Literature and The Indian Elite." *Cornell Journal of Social Relations.* 1, No. 1 (1966), 25-32.

Verghese, C. Paul. "Indian English and Man in Indo-Anglian Fiction." *Indian Literature.* 14, No. 1 (1970).

... "*The Coffer Dams*" (Reviewed). *Indian Writing Today.* 4, No. 4 (Oct.-Nov. 1970), 237.

Venkatachari, K. "Sense of life in Kamala Markandaya's *Nectar in a Sieve.*" *Osmania Journal of English Studies.* 9, No. 1 (1972), 55-59.

Venkateswaran, Shyamala. "The Language of Kamala Markandaya's Novels." *Literary Criterion.* 9, No. 3 (Winter, 1970), 57-67.

INDEX